Th. Jefferson

THE DEBT PENALTY

By Richard E. McConnell
Illustrated by Barbara L. Curran

LIBRARY OF CONGRESS CATALOG CARD NUMBER: 91-91155
ISBN 0-9630852-0-4

PRINTED IN THE UNITED STATES OF AMERICA

To my dad

PREFACE

My father once asked me what I wanted to be when I grew up. I told him, not surprisingly, that I wasn't sure. He suggested that if ever I did discover the answer to his question, to write him outlining my goals.

I never wrote that letter.

Forty years passed and it is now too late to write him. In fact, I have always known the answer to his question, and I think he would have been pleased, but I never had the nerve or the presumption to reveal it to him. I simply wanted to be as good as my father. That was a goal, I knew, I could not achieve although even today I still try.

Quite recently, I started writing about my father, revealing his thoughts and experiences told to me over a forty year period. They include some of his investment ideas that are as applicable today as they were in his time.

This book is a collection of those lessons portraying the world scene as I see it guided in part by a father's influence. I hope my first book will interest and amuse you. If it does, I shall have achieved a goal I have long hoped for; to entertain and instruct a patient reader while paying respect to a teacher, a father and a friend.

NOTES FROM THE AUTHOR

THE DEBT PENALTY is my first book about debt accumulation and the coming American Tragedy. I was guided in writing it by lessons my father taught me. My interpretation of current events in this book is influenced strongly by him.

In later chapters, I discuss an investment program for my family and friends that may be a solution to the investment dilemma facing all Americans in the nineties. It is my first look at emerging nations, their awakening economies, and the investment opportunities present there.

My final chapter is a description of my estate plan which I decided at the last moment to mention in passing. After all, any good investment plan should consider the consequences of death, especially someone my age.

TABLE OF CONTENTS

CHANGING HORSES

To lose an important client in the investment business is a real downer. The news of a dismissal spreads around and usually implies unsatisfactory performance.

Last summer my firm lost one of its oldest and best clients, despite what I thought were excellent results. It was a big reversal. Our client had been persuaded to switch to a growth stock manager who happened to be a friend of mine.

No sooner had the new manager been appointed and the new portfolio set in place than the growth stock sector of the market collapsed. The devastation to the portfolio took place with incredible speed.

The incident was similar to an episode that occurred 60 years ago to my father. It reminded me of that old adage about changing horses in the middle of a stream.

When my father returned from naval duty after World War I, he went to work for Colonel Seeley Mudd, a successful mining engineer. Colonel Mudd founded Texas Gulf Sulfur and had a lead role in the financing of Alaska Juneau, Cyprus Mines, and Mesabi Iron. There were many other ventures with which he was identified.

In most of his ventures, Dad's boss had three well known financial partners: W.B. Thompson, founder of Newmont Mining Co.; Bernard M. Baruch, a wealthy Wall Street investor; and Herbert Hoover, a distinguished civil servant. Colonel Mudd's endorsement of my dad's acumen was sufficient to gain Dad the ear and respect of the other partners.

As time passed and my father became more experienced, he was sent to New York City to open a brokerage house for Colonel Mudd. Thompson, Baruch, and Hoover were a few of the firm's list of illustrious clients. The idea was to advise in the investment of mining stocks.

By 1929, Colonel Mudd had passed away and Dad had become one of Herbert Hoover's personal investment managers. It was an awesome responsibility for a young man in his thirties. The relationship with President Hoover was cordial, but always rather formal. That was Mr. Hoover's way. President Hoover often invited members of his cabinet and advisors to his fishing camp in Little Washington, Virginia. The summer White House was an ideal fishing and riding vacation home.

One Saturday morning in June, 1929, a select group of guests rode in single file behind the President as he climbed the steep mountain trails on his horse. From time to time he would summon one of his guests to ride up along side him so that he could review developments with his advisor.

After his talk with the President, Secretary of War Patrick Hurley rode back to the end of the column. He was a handsome military figure, popular at most social affairs in Washington.

"The President wants to see you Robert," he said to my father as he pulled up. "He's in a good mood."

Dad rode up ahead. He was quite nervous.

The President seemed especially cordial "Bob, tell me what you've been up to," he queried.

Dad hesitated, "Mr. President," he began, "I don't like the looks of things. I have liquidated the partnership assets for the time being until I see new opportunities." There was a long silence. The President rode forward, his face not visible, yet Dad sensed his anger.

"I guess that means you have no confidence in my Administration," said Hoover caustically. My father did not reply. They rode on for several more minutes in silence. Finally, the President spoke. He avoided my dad's face.

"Would you ask Secretary Mellon to join me as you go back, Robert?"

My father did as he was told. It was the last time President Hoover ever spoke to him.

The next week Dad sailed on an ocean liner for Southhampton, England. He was exhausted and dejected to have lost his most prestigious client; the President of the United States had fired him.

Bernard Baruch was on board. "I understand your firm lost a

good account,'' said Baruch. It sounded as though he was gloating.

''Yes, sir,'' my father replied sullenly.

''Well I'm staying with you,'' said Baruch, ''I think you're right.''

Three months later in September '29 Wall Street crashed. Dad was right.

Like I said, losing a good client really hurts, especially when your judgment is the correct one. Very often it hurts the client as well.

THE BRONZE AGE

When my father was working for Colonel Seeley Mudd in 1924, he was asked if he would like to participate in a mining venture Colonel Mudd was financing. Colonel Mudd was a legendary figure, a very successful investor and my dad was pleased to have been asked to invest in his copper mining enterprise.

A commodity crash in the late twenties caused acute losses at the mines. The coming of World War II interrupted the mining operations entirely a few years later. So it was not until 1947 that the venture, known as Cyprus Mines, became a profit center after twenty five years of patient investing.

In 1962, forty years had passed, and my father sold his interest at a substantial profit; 10,000 times his investment. That's patience! That's profit!

The story of the founding of Cyprus Mines deserves mention as well. As with most important discoveries, chance played a major role.

Colonel Seeley Mudd was introduced to an archaeologist, a student of antiquity in the early 20's. Dr. Gunther, the archaeologist, was interested in locating the original source of copper that was the raw material basis of the Bronze Age. He was convinced that the site of the world's first operating copper deposit was somewhere in the eastern Mediterranean. This site he believed would be recognizable by the green hue that copper pyrites imparts to the soil. He believed that primitive man had been curious about the earth's green discoloration and ultimately figured out how to smelt the visible copper from its ore with fire. Gunther's studies concluded that huge amounts of copper were mined by Phoenician slave labor in open pit mines about 2000 B.C.

Colonel Mudd was intrigued. Soon after he heard the story, he financed Gunther's search in the eastern Mediterranean.

For several months, Dr. Gunther traveled searching for a further clue to the location of these ancient mines.

Nearly a year had passed when Gunther, tired and unsuccessful, received a cable from Colonel Mudd, suggesting they call off the search. He read and reread this disheartening message aloud on the porch of the old Shepherd's Hotel in Alexandria, Egypt. An elderly gentleman sitting next to him, an Egyptian, listened patiently. He suggested to his new American acquaintance that he visit the Island of Cyprus on his way home to America, where he might see an area similar to the one Gunther described.

Less than a month later, Gunther cabled Colonel Mudd that he had found an ancient mine site on the Island of Cyprus. After months of extensive excavation financed by Mudd and his partners, the mines were reactivated after laying dormant 4,000 years. Early relics of Phoenician civilization were found in the ruins and presented by the surviving children of Colonel Mudd to museums and colleges.

My father told me this story and commented that he did not understand why Dr. Gunther had not gone first to the Island of

Cyprus to commence his search. "After all," he said, "the word Cyprus is the Greek word for 'copper'. I would have thought an archaeologist, like Gunther, would have known that, wouldn't you?"

"Isn't it amazing," he added, "how often something very obvious is hardest of all to see?"

THE CHEAPEST AIRLINE

Whenever I suggested an investment idea to my dad, he was remarkably patient before he responded. I wish I could be that patient. More often than not he rejected my thoughts, but with encouragement, and a phrase I have come to use as my own. "Dick, I like your idea and I think it is interesting," he would say, "but it is not compelling."

I came to adopt this philosophy myself in later years and I find even today that a "compelling" investment is the only kind.

Let me tell you of an example that came to my attention nearly thirty years ago.

I remember the introductory sentence to my first research report written for my Wall Street employer in 1963. It was an evaluation of American Express Company after a much publicized scandal involving its salad oil division.

"What is it," I asked, "you can make for ten cents, sell for ten dollars, and when the buyer uses it, charge him a dime?" I was referring to the credit card. This was the beginning of my study of a company that appeared to be in serious trouble.

In 1963, American Express Company revealed to its startled shareholders that it had suffered an indeterminate, but substantial loss. Tony DiAngelis, a trusted employee from Bayonne, New Jersey, cleverly drained the salad oil vats of American Express, under his charge, for his own account, in an ingenious way. He nailed the outside indicators of these huge vats to the "full" position so that no one suspected the containers were being emptied by Mr. DiAngelis. That is, not until someone climbed up to the top of one of these great vats and peered in.

When this naughty deed was revealed with full press coverage to the investing public, investors sent American Express stock retreating to half its prior deserved value — no kidding, from $70/share to $35. Most stockholders didn't even know the company had a salad oil division. Indeed, the directors suffered a similar embarrassment.

Meanwhile, as these press reports brought disappointment to the company's shareholders and the stock's price, the credit card division was busily introducing to all the world's airlines a new concept. The credit card public was offered a "fly now, pay later" plan that was a first in the airline industry, and of course, for American Express.

During this period, I interviewed directors and employees of the company, as well as airline officials. I made estimates about growth in the number of card holders and card use based on estimated future airline traffic. I visited the only serious credit card competitor of American Express and found it hopelessly bogged down with newly installed IBM equipment that didn't work. It appeared to me that American Express had the credit card airline market to itself, and I believed that this was a great growth opportunity for the company. I also became convinced that the estimates of loss of the salad oil division were vastly overstated by an imaginative press. With great excitement and pride, I finished my work and titled it "American Express Company, The Cheapest Airline."

My employer was not as pleased as I with my revelations. He feared a subject of such controversy might backfire and suggested I defer the publication of my report. He wasn't sure of my facts either, he told me. I found out later he bought American Express stock for himself, without telling me.

I swallowed my disappointment, crossed the street to 115 Broadway for lunch, and told a friend my sad story. He bought 184,000 shares for his principals and later asked me to join his firm as President. I then went over to see Howard Stein at Dreyfus Corporation. He also bought the stock; he accumulated 9% of the outstanding shares of the company and became its largest shareholder.

There have been many other instances when the price of a stock falls to low valuations while its earnings prospects improve. It happens in mundane industries where pleasant surprises are rare, as well as in more glamorous environments.

I remember DeBeers after the Sharpville incident; Disney after the death of its founder; Philip Morris after the Surgeon General's report on lung cancer; Federal National Mortgage in the money crunch of 1982. There have really been a number of them. I can think of a few going on today. It's one way to search for a compelling value and I recommend it. So does my dad.

INSTRUMENT LANDINGS

I must tell a story of my only close encounter with stock charts.

I have been confused and consequently annoyed most of my career by the wide use of charts in the investment process. I used to think chartists were too lazy to do basic research and were in a class with card readers, astrologers and crystal ball gazers.

But that all changed for me briefly in 1963, when I was ushered into the offices of Howard Stein of Dreyfus Corporation. Mr. Stein was Chairman and long time head of this prestigious multi-billion dollar investment firm in New York City. My appointment with him was arranged to discuss my research work on American Express Company after that company's so-called "salad oil scandal."

Mr. Stein was on the floor of his carpeted office intently studying a very large chart of Union Oil of California. He and his investment associate, Kenny Oberman, were considering the purchase of Union Oil stock. Mr. Stein's final decision seemed to be resting on the chart he was staring at and the message it imparted to him.

That was the day I determined to study charts and review my long term prejudice against them. If they were good enough for Mr. Stein of Dreyfus Corporation, they ought to be vital to me.

Since that time, I have come to view charts in the same manner a stunt pilot might view his instrument panel. His instruments are a valuable guide to the decisions he must make, but he prefers, instinctively, to rely on his five senses.

There is no doubt, however, that charts are widely used and are a major factor in determining stock prices — a very major factor. This is true despite the fact that they are often subject to widely disparate interpretations, and are even used by professional managers who profess not to use them at all.

There must be fifty books published on the reading of charts and the technical aspects of the market. Technicians or chartists, I would guess, have a greater short-term impact on market behavior than important economic events or dramatic research revelations. I seem to remember that Joe Granville, a chartist legend at one time, was personally responsible for a market collapse.

So it's not surprising to find most of the research directors of Wall Street incorporating in their economic forecast, supportive data from the firm's technical director. My partners try to read much of this valuable research work as it is published; but I, for one, tend to skip over the charts. Despite my unwitting prejudice, I have copied below two charts that you can study at your convenience; one of Union Oil which Mr. Stein was studying and the other of American Express. You don't have to be a Rhodes scholar to see which company stock has had the superior price performance. To be fair to Howard Stein and his chart reading proclivities, I should mention that Dreyfus Corporation purchased a major position in the outstanding stock of American Express shortly after my visit, and became its largest shareholder.

I often wonder what Mr. Stein saw in the chart of American Express that caused him to move with such confidence.

As for flying, I for one still prefer visual flight regulations to instrument landings.

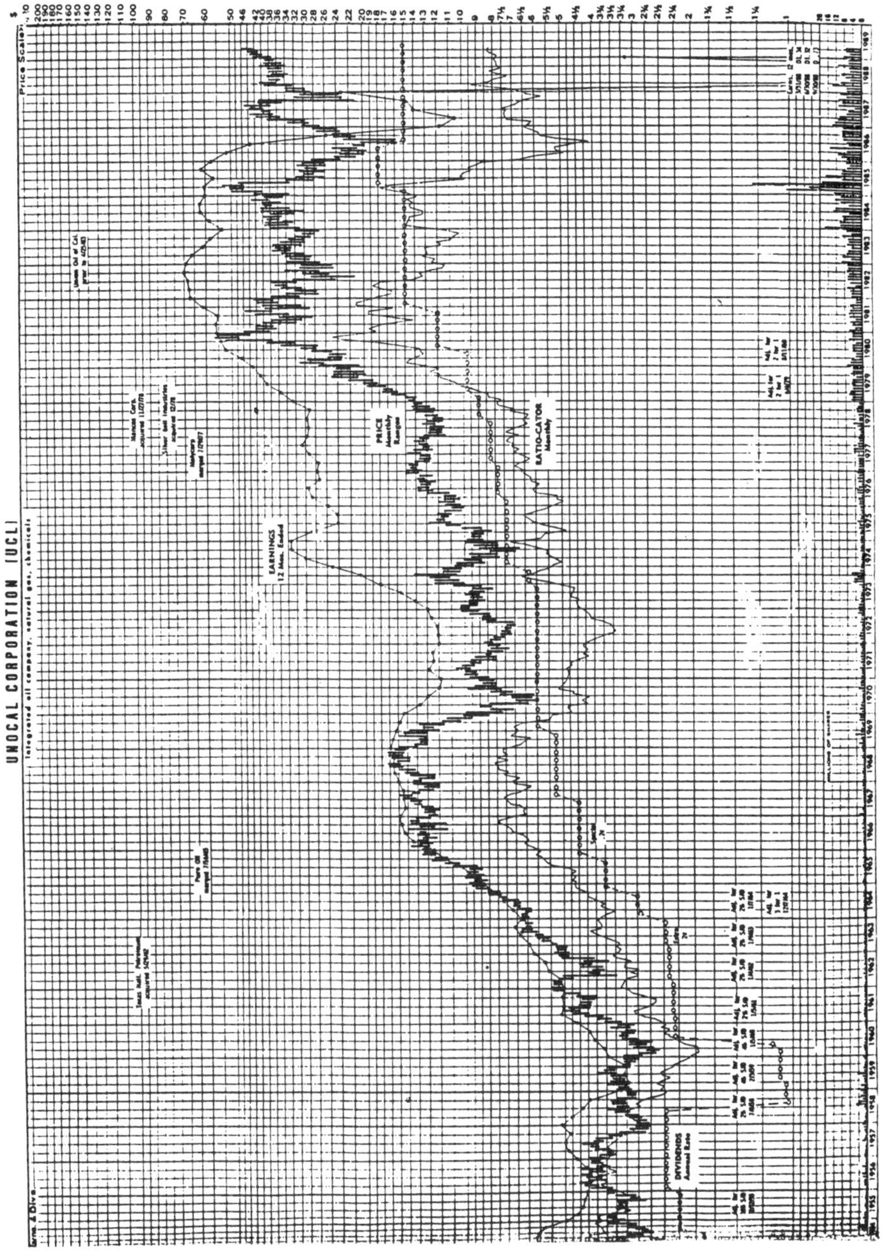
UNOCAL CORPORATION (UCL)
Integrated oil company, natural gas, chemicals
Price Scale
EARNINGS
12 Mos. Ended
PRICE
Monthly
Ranges
RATIO-CATOR
Monthly
DIVIDENDS
Annual Rate

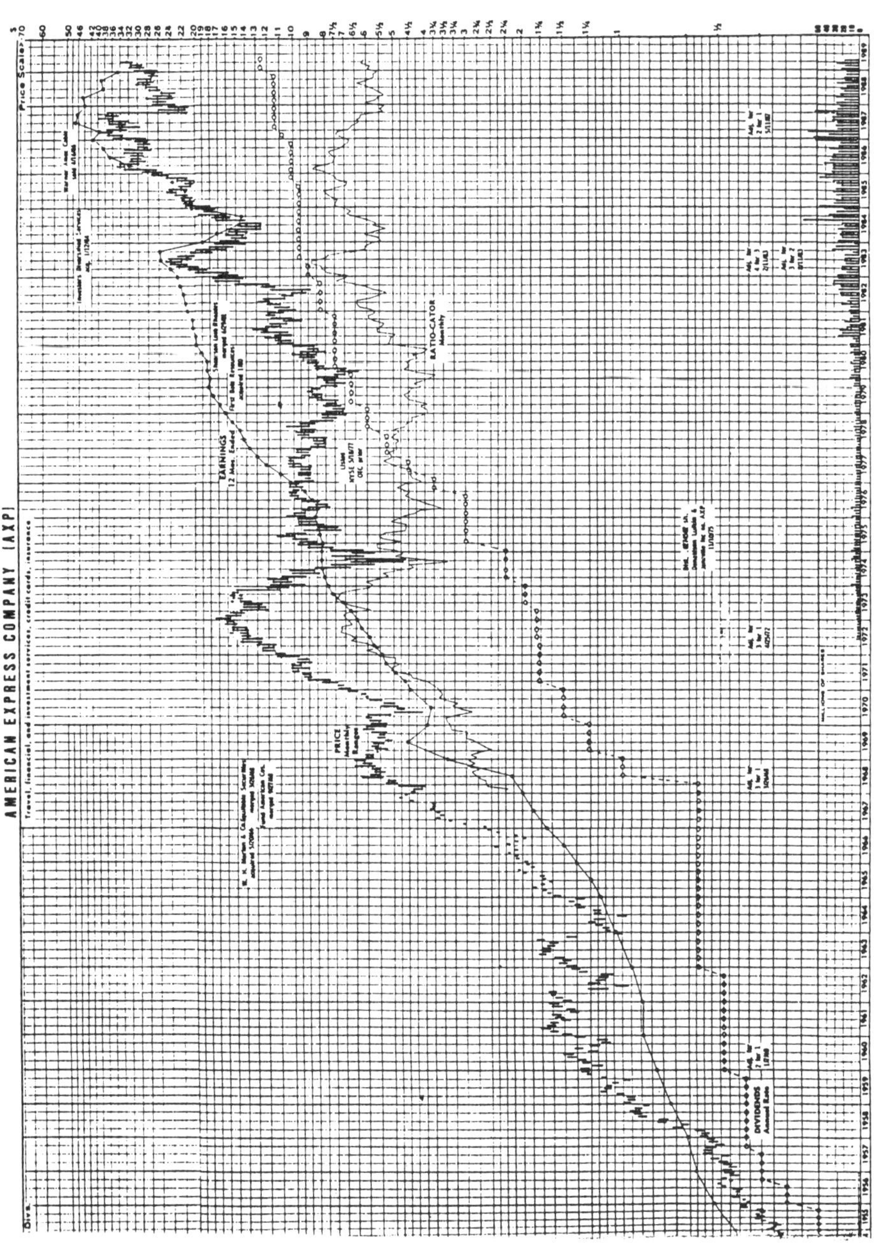
AMERICAN EXPRESS COMPANY (AXP)
Travel, financial, and investment services, credit cards, insurance
EARNINGS
12 Mos. Ended
PRICE
Monthly Ranges
DIVIDENDS
Annual Rate
RATIO-CATOR
Monthly
Price Scale

NATURE'S WAY

Dad was a great admirer of Thomas Jefferson. He considered him America's first environmentalist. I think people, unlike Jefferson, are too pessimistic about our environment and the damage being done to it today. Things may not be as bad as they think. I'll tell you why.

I had an Israeli friend who came for a weekend visit to our house in Virginia. We lived on a golf course in Charlottesville overlooking the fifteenth hole, a long par five. It was springtime and the country was lush and green.

My friend, David, stared at the expanse of green foliage and grass that surrounded our home. It was so different a sight from the one to which he was accustomed in Israel.

"It's not just the green grass," he said, "it's the ponds and streams that are scattered everywhere around this beautiful area. In my home, grass and flowing water don't exist."

David hasn't been back in the U.S. in many years. He is running a company in Tel Aviv now, but I am reminded of his comment so often when I read how our fresh water resources have been polluted.

My father used to say that grass was one of nature's ways for storing water for man's use. However you look at it, water is an essential part of our well-being and one of the most neglected natural resources. Revelations of the pollution along the waterways of the world are very discouraging to me, especially the recent reports of the devastation in eastern Europe. The United States is in pretty bad shape as well.

They tell me the citizens of Memphis, Tennessee drink water that has passed at least four times through the toilet bowls of their northern neighbors. Not long ago, in Cleveland, one of the downtown rivers caught fire from floating chemical pollutants. In Sacramento, California, the irrigation water has become saline.

The water table through overuse and drought has fallen 60 feet in 1990 alone. It has been falling for years. It's a messy scene no matter where you look and a problem that will plague us for many years to come. We have been squandering much of our natural wealth for too long. So it is comforting to see young people trying to stop this abuse.

In keeping with my long term optimism, let mention the remarks I heard by a leading environmentalist. He pointed out three serious areas of pollution of the postwar era that are now greatly improved. In each case the cure was merely a commitment by citizens to discontinue their neglectful ways.

His first example was the rancid air and choking smog of the City of London. For years, dating back to Sherlock Holmes and Dr. Watson, the air was foul with soot from the chimney pots of London. By city ordinance in 1949, Londoners were forbidden the use of coal in the heating of their homes. Today, London's air is clean, cleaner than any time in memory. What's more, London homes are warm at last; the owners use gas.

Secondly, the speaker mentioned the New York City garbage site at Idlewild, a rat infested, diseased area of more than a thousand acres. By prohibiting the disposal of refuse at this site a few years ago, Idlewild is now a renowned bird sanctuary for migrating water fowl. Take a look out the window on your next flight from JFK. It's possible you'll see a bird watcher.

Lastly, he mentioned Lake Washington, a small resort in the far West that had been abandoned by its 300 residents because they had polluted the lake with their raw sewage and indiscriminate abuse of their lake. The children of that community's residents banded together to build a central sewage plant for the homes in the area and simultaneously banned the dumping of refuse. Today, Lake Washington's water is crystal clear, restocked with sport fish.

In each case, the only measure needed to clean up the polluted area was the decision to stop polluting. Mother Nature quickly restored the air, the land, and the water each to its former use and beauty. That's nature's way.

We may be only a generation away from a clean and healthful environment once we accept that message. It's already accepted in so many places and I hope it's accepted where you live.

THE WAR AGAINST PROGRESS

My mother's great uncle was Thomas Hardy. He was author of many severe books of fiction depicting life in England in the 19th Century. I now have the complete works of this great author. These volumes help me realize the economic progress that has occurred since this famous man chronicled the hard life in England he knew, more than a century ago.

There was pollution, crime and poverty then; not unlike conditions found today. Human cruelty and kindness were closely proportioned as they are today; apparently increasing wealth in the intervening years did not change the proportions these ingredients share on planet Earth. True progress has been a slow learner while rising income has been an overachieving student.

In recent years, a new wealthy generation of protestants are changing all that. A unique breed of self-motivated adherents using their time and determination to increase the slow speed of real progress.

Fear for man's future has produced these "green peace" citizens. They have the education, the income and iniative to fight for a new order.

Ralph Nader was probably the first visible member of this cult. He still is the leader of a cadre of battle-hardened dreamers who share one thing in common, the crusade against all man-made abuses.

They were the first to protest oil spills, chemical wastes, insecticides and air pollution; child abuse, wife abuse, and the homeless; the whale, the wolf and a broad spectrum of endangered species. The subjects of their attention expanded to reach every perceived social wrong. What's more, miraculously, they became highly effective. Their insolence and their intolerance reached the highest levels. They no longer can be ignored. They are a new-sprung Society of Don Quixotes, once laughed at even scorned, but now applauded.

If Thomas Hardy were alive today, he might well be penning the story of power of these unpaid few who are winning the war against progress. These are embarrassing offspring of a world in the process of cleaning up the thoughtless acts of their ancestors.

If Divine Providence is somewhere watching the passing events today on His Planet Earth, He most assuredly must be pleased.

THE STREETS OF BELLE GLADE

I remember many experiences with my father. He was a great teacher, especially economic subjects.

He told me, as a young boy, about Pharaoh's dream from the Old Testament and Joseph's forecast of seven years of famine. Dad wasn't teaching Bible stories, he was teaching economics. He wanted me to know about economic cycles.

During the late 1930's, my father purchased a farm near Cambridge, Maryland at the mouth of the Choptank River; one of his crops was tomatoes. He and I drove there from Washington, D.C. one August morning.

On the main road from Easton to Cambridge, we approached the huge Phillips Packing Plant, the only canning facility on the Eastern shore. In front of us, as we arrived, was a veritable mountain of tomatoes that could be seen on the flat terrain for miles around.

Dad stopped the car and we both got out and tasted an abandoned ripe tomato from the pile. They were delicious.

My father explained: "This year we have had the best tomato harvest in memory. We couldn't have asked for a better crop. But Phillips Packing hasn't been able to get financing from the bank to can any more tomatoes, the markets are flooded; so Mr. Phillips told all the growers in the area he wouldn't accept any more product. Many of the local farmers were angry; so angry they dumped their tomatoes on Phillips' front field."

I ate another tomato as we drove on. It was very good, but it was a bad year for tomatoes.

Years later, after World War II, Dad bought a cattle ranch near Belle Glade, Florida, 3000 acres of St. Augustine grasslands. We often drove to the ranch from Jupiter Island about 70 miles away.

On one occasion, he decided to take me to the Belle Glade cattle auction, which was held every Saturday morning. It was the year that Ezra Taft Benson was Secretary of Agriculture in the Eisenhower administration. Cattle prices were very low; it was the bottom of a cycle.

An old rancher from nearby Clewiston drove into town with a load of cattle that day. Apparently the price for beef had just reached a seven year low, 6 cents/per pound. He was disgusted. Rather than take his loss on the eighteen steers he had brought to town in his truck, the old farmer released them to run wild in the streets of Belle Glade.

His picture was on the front page of the local paper the very next day. He was arrested for disturbing the peace. He looked angry!

I asked Dad what Secretary Benson proposed to do about the surplus of feeder cattle.

"Nothing," he said glumly, "Benson says we have to eat our way out of it."

Belle Glade has gone downhill since then; today its called "The AIDS capitol of the South." It's a big drug trafficking town. The cattle business is secondary, the ranchers say it's too cyclical. There aren't many truck farmers or cattle ranchers out there like there were forty years ago. It's mostly sugar plantation.

People today are more apt to be in industry or at a desk job. More likely they trade stocks and bonds or some of the new instruments if they are really serious; things like tigers, cats, calls, and warrants. Dozens of new derivative products have been created in the stock market these days. People don't own tomato farms or cattle ranches anymore; they trade intangibles not tomatoes.

Well, I hope things never get as bad as they did when Dad was alive. Can you imagine if one day no one would buy your intangibles; like my Dad's cattle or tomatoes; not even bid for them? What would you do then?

Have you ever eaten a put, or swallowed a call?

MILITARY INTELLIGENCE

One of the best books I ever read about the investment process was "The Battle for Investment Survival" by Jerald Loeb. It's out of print now, but if you see a copy, pick it up. Even its title is timely in today's market of occasional war jitters.

Speaking of war, I think army officers and investment managers share a similar responsibility and often make similar errors. I had an experience 48 years ago that brought me to this conclusion.

I trained at Fort Benning, Georgia in 1943 before being assigned to the 397th infantry regiment of the 100th Division. In late October, our division shipped out from Camp Kilmer for a crossing that we all wrongly supposed was England. We landed in Marseilles, France eleven days later.

After three weeks of trucking and marching, we found ourselves in the foothills of the Vosges Mountains pursuing the slow retreat of the German Army. The weather was cold and wet.

Our advance through tree covered hills and occasional narrow open valleys was interrupted by mortar and artillery attacks from hidden German emplacements. Casualties were high.

On the first day of clear weather, our battalion of 800 remaining men emerged into a broad valley divided by a narrow paved road. We walked down the hill comforted by the sight of large numbers of U.S. tanks and field pieces in close formation on the road below.

Obviously we were winning and the Germans had withdrawn.

I spoke to one of the tank commanders and asked if he could spare some bread and peanut butter for a sandwich from his provisions that were strapped to his tank. He consented, and I was soon munching my lunch peacefully. I had not eaten in 24 hours.

The next thing I remember was a deafening explosion and a sickening pain in both my legs. A mortar shell had landed directly behind me and had thrown me into the air with a force that simultaneously flipped a passing officer's jeep. The scene was like a chicken house after a shotgun blast.

That was the end of the war for me. I was transported back from one hospital to another until my final discharge from Walter Reed Hospital one year later.

Looking back in memory on that experience, I realize our field commander made a stupid mistake. He was informed that the Germans had made a complete withdrawal, and he believed it. He didn't verify his information. He didn't order his soldiers to disperse in case he was wrong.

He probably should have been court martialed, but that wasn't to be. I heard later that he and his driver were in the jeep that passed me that fateful moment. Both men were killed.

The experience confirmed for me the accuracy of German artillery at point blank range as well as my prejudice against inexperienced officers.

There are investment officers today, like my battalion commander, who have not faced adverse conditions; they are green. Many of them are found in bank trust departments with important titles. Few of them survive in the battle for investment survival.

If I were choosing a professional investment manager for myself, I would check his results during severe periods. During such periods he learns his trade. If he performs well then, he probably will do well in the future. It's not enough that he outperforms the Dow, he must also avoid unnecessary losses.

THE PAJAMA GAME

At church one Sunday, someone was reading from the Old Testament, and I thought I heard a story about Abraham, who was about to set fire to his son Isaac, as a sacrifice to God. I awoke with a start.

The story of Abraham in the Old Testament reminded me of a story concerning my father.

I may have mentioned my brief encounter with the enemy in World War II. My injuries and rehabilitation were a costly affair for everyone involved, except the enemy.

After my return to Walter Reed Hospital in Washington, D.C., my military career came to an end. The medical authorities determined my legs would not improve, and I was discharged on a Friday in May on crutches with a recommended compensation award of $22/month. I was still a teenager.

At that time, my father was an assistant secretary of the Treasury under Henry Morganthau. His assignment was the drafting of a plan for the reconstruction of Germany after hostilities had ceased. While the war had not yet ended, surrender was imminent, and the ailing President Roosevelt needed a plan to implement when the surrender occurred.

While Dad was an engineer first, an economist second, he was convinced that the health of the German economy after World War II was essential to the well-being of postwar Europe. As an engineer, he also argued strongly that Germany could not wage modern war against its neighbors, if denied the essential sinews of war. These important raw materials-aluminum, sulfur, and petroleum—(the essential sinews of war) were not available in Germany except through importation. Without them, he argued, Germany was no threat. He believed the United States could control Germany's imports.

Dad's work was presented to the Treasury Department's senior staff the week before I was discharged from the Walter Reed Hospital.

Harry Dexter White was also an assistant secretary of the Treasury under Morganthau and part of the top staff. Unbeknownst to Dad, White had taken it upon himself to write his own reconstruction plan for Germany. He did this, in part, to counteract my father's plan and, in part, to please Secretary Morganthau. It was called the Agrarian Report or Morganthau Plan.

I was surprised with the suddenness with which I was discharged from Walter Reed Hospital on this special day. I was taken by military vehicle to meet my father at the Treasury Department. It was Friday, and we normally drove out to the farm in Middleburg, Virginia for the weekend. But this day I didn't even have time to change into street clothes. I was still in my pajamas, slippers, and bathrobe when I was summoned by the officer of the day at the hospital, and told I was leaving immediately.

My driver stopped at the Treasury, I got out on crutches and was greeted by my father at the entrance. He said we were going to meet Secretary Morganthau. I blanched. I was in Army issue pajamas.

We went up one flight to a spacious hallway slowly and walked to the Secretary's outer office.

An overweight man, whose crutches leaned against the wall, greeted my father and me. He was Morganthau's personal assistant, a polio victim. He acted as though all of my father's guests arrived in their bathrobes.

There were five men in all in the grand office; Secretary Morganthau, Undersecretary Dan Bell, Assistant Secretaries Ed Foley, Bill O'Donnell, and Harry Dexter White.

The Secretary was cordial and businesslike. "We are just discussing your father's plan for the reconstruction of Germany, Richard," he said. He then spoke to his staff, "I wonder if all of you gentlemen here have had a chance to read it?" They all nodded. "Good," he said. "Then does anyone have any questions or comments?"

Harry Dexter White was a slight, balding man with a pale scaly complexion. He looked overworked. White commenced. "Mr. Secretary, I have read McConnell's report, and it is apparent he wants to rebuild Germany."

There was an awesome silence.

My father, to me, had always been a tall, impressive man. He rose from his seat opposite White who was next to me on the couch. He towered over us both. "Mr. Secretary," Dad's voice trembled, "there are more than two hundred reasons why I do not want to rebuild Germany's war power; all of them are in my son's legs!" As he spoke, his face reddened.

Mr. Morganthau held up his hand as his phone rang. He disliked heated discussions. He spoke graciously and briefly on the phone for a moment and then hung up. "It's Friday gentlemen," said Morganthau, "why don't we continue on Monday with this discussion?"

He then smiled at me as he rose and said, "Richard, what do you think of your father's plan?"

My throat was dry and I felt very small in a room full of giants. I answered, "I'll be glad when it's over, Sir, and everyone has quit fighting." The meeting ended, and I was ushered out on crutches, in my bathrobe, followed by my father.

Morganthau's personal secretary shook my hand as we left. He said "I hope you get rid of those crutches soon Richard, I'd sure like to get rid of mine. Good-bye."

We climbed into Dad's Lincoln Zephyr and headed for home. Dad was still bristling. He disliked Mr. White, I could tell that. "You did fine, Dick," he said. "I guess you noticed that the phone rang before I could get really mad. That's because that crippled fellow listens in. He's Morganthau's assistant. Every time there's a fight, he rings the phone in the Secretary's office." We drove on the rest of the way in silence. It was good to be going home.

Well that's my secret; that was the day Dad's Engineer's Report prevailed over Harry Dexter White's Agrarian Report, and I was there. Although I didn't find out until much later, Dad's argument was strong enough to prevail.

I still have a hunch he planned the whole meeting and used me as one of his props like a sacrificial lamb, like Isaac, but I don't care. I think he did the right thing.

ROCKS

I was admitted to Princeton University in 1945. I was the first returned wounded veteran of World War II. While I did not realize it at the time, my crutches gave me a preferred status as a student that I desperately needed, otherwise I might never have graduated.

What I best remember of those days, however, has nothing to do with my studies. My story relates to another student, a graduate student, at the School for Advanced Studies. His name was Albert Einstein.

Adelaide DeLong was the only child of Professor and Mrs. DeLong and the only girl I knew at Princeton in my first year. She was seventeen years old and in her last year of high school. We were good friends. Adelaide lived not far from Holder Hall, my dormitory, and next door to Albert Einstein and his sister. When she was a bit younger, Adelaide often visited the Einstein's on her way back from school and shared her jelly beans with them. In return, Dr. Einstein helped with her math homework.

In early summer of 1945, Dr. Einstein was little more than an eccentric German scholar to me. $E=mc^2$ was still a mysterious formula in those days known only to physicists at the School for Advanced Studies. But after the atomic explosions in Japan, and the Japanese surrender, all that changed. Dr. Einstein appeared on the cover of Time Magazine with a mushroom cloud in the background. He suddenly became the man of the hour — famous nationwide and worldwide — and he was all ours.

If the world had changed in its appraisal of Einstein, it wasn't noticeable in his household. Dr. Einstein's sister still guarded and cared for him without assistance. She prepared his meals, laundered his clothes, and accompanied him on his short walks to the village. Moreover, Adelaide and I were still welcome.

Dr. Einstein was usually seated in a high backed chair in a corner of his living room, with a strong reading light behind him. He wore the top to a gray gym suit, sandals, and unpressed pants.

I found the reading light behind him a bit strange, never mind his informal attire, because so far as I knew, he did not read. No, no, I mean it. He just sat and thought. There were no books visible in his house.

When Adelaide and I came to call, his sister always welcomed us, then left briefly to fetch Dr. Einstein his long stemmed white clay pipe and tobacco. In a moment, he had tapped some tobacco into the small bowl. Clouds of smoke rose from his pipe slowly toward the light above him until I imagined the cover of Time with Einstein's benign face staring out at me from a menacing mushroom cloud.

On one evening in August, I was very close to his chair seated cross-legged on the floor, my crutches nearby. I enjoyed the aroma of his pipe.

"Dr. Einstein," I asked, "when did you first think of your formula $E=mc^2$?"

"Ven I vas nine," he replied. "I vas staying with my grandmother and I vondered vat it vould be like to run as fast as the light from her gas lamp and look down."

Years later, in a book by Bronowski called THE ASCENT OF MAN, the statement was repeated verbatim by the author, except Einstein apparently said he was fourteen when he first thought of his revolutionary formula.

I suppose the good Doctor decided on a later date because he thought no one would believe him if he told the truth.

Shortly after that evening meeting, Einstein agreed to speak at a Whig-Clio Society monthly assembly. I was lucky enough to have asked him to be our guest speaker before his public schedule became intolerable for him.

It was early September when he addressed an audience of students and professors. It was very warm that evening. There was no air conditioning in our overcrowded auditorium, and the speech was difficult to follow because of his thick German accent which detracted from his message. His audience, understandably, had difficulty remaining alert.

At the close of his talk, there was polite applause; students were then invited to ask questions.

Dr. Einstein recognized a student's raised arm.

"Sir," the student began, "what do you believe will be the weapons of World War III?"

"I don't know," our guest replied, "But I know vat the veapons of Vorld Var IV will be — ROCKS!"

The audience roared with laughter believing his remark a hysterical joke. Everyone laughed except the speaker. He was not amused.

A GIRL'S BEST FRIEND

The recent death of my cousin, whom I have known and loved from childhood, was a loss for me. He was a real friend. His passing reminds me of an incident in my life that I treasure.

In 1961, I had a desk job in New York City investigating opportunities for a small west coast mining company. I had tried a couple of my ideas on the management without success. I soon tired of being in the east alone and ignored. I began wondering about a career change, but decided to make one more try before giving up.

I wrote a final and very brief letter to my boss in the fall of 1961.

"What company," I questioned, "is a household name, a worldwide monopoly, sells below net current assets, at 3 times earnings, at 2 times cash flow, with no long or short term debt, $1 billion in assets, an 11 percent dividend yield; 10 percent earnings growth, 17 million shares outstanding, and you won't buy it?"

Sincerely yours, Dick.

The letter, though most surely in poor taste, did bring a prompt response. A few days later I received a phone call from my boss.

"Dick," he said, "I have a feeling you're in the wrong job. You should be on Wall Street."

I was never certain, not to this day, whether I had been fired in a friendly way or had merely been given good advice; but in any case, a few weeks later I took his advice and moved to a brokerage office at 120 Broadway. My boss became my first client.

The Company that I alluded to, in my brief letter, was one of the largest mining houses in the world, which among other things controlled the world's diamond trade, DeBeers Consolidated Mines. Indeed, it was and is today a household name and worldwide monopoly.

Its stock had fallen in price that summer following a black African uprising that came to be known as the Sharpville incident. The civil trouble was put down abruptly by the white minority government amid world wide criticism of South Africa's brutal treatment of its black population. The British Government issued a formal protest. In response, South Africa withdrew from the British Commonwealth of Nations and simultaneously took strong measures to restrict the flow of funds leaving the country.

Stock values on the Johannesburg Stock Exchange fell dramatically. DeBeers, whose stock was widely held and traded, was especially hard hit.

Despite what first appeared to be the beginning of the white supremacy Government's overthrow, the Sharpville incident was not repeated; things returned to normal. The Johannesburg market recovered from its fright. DeBeers stock rose in value four times in less than two years from its depressed low.

No one was more surprised than I at its dramatic rise, but it remained an important part of my memory. It was the first time I had ever spoken out and been right. It was also my first exposure to a phenomenon that I have come to witness many times since.

A fully publicized, nonrecurring and dramatic event frightens shareholders into selling their stockholdings, (like the Sharpville Incident), while the earning power of the company remains intact. The entire round trip event or opportunity is rarely more than a few months in duration, but it is, nevertheless, an occurrence, that, over the years, is far more frequent than you might imagine. If you try I am sure you can remember many occasions of your own.

I mention this incident because it was a turning point for me in my career and I am pleased it was a good one. What's more, I can happily blame it on my boss, my friend, my cousin.

I'll miss him.

CALL FOR PHILIP MORRIS

My father graduated from Columbia School of Mines in 1904. His first assignment was running a lead mine in the Colorado mountains. While snowed in, the men under his direction prepared the mine for summer operations, and in the spring they dug out and skied to a valley mining town 1400 feet below. They often ran out of important supplies like sugar and cigarettes.

The craving for sugar was paramount to them, and the need for tobacco almost as great. They drank quantities of sarsaparilla, a drink like root beer, as soon as they arrived in the village. After their sugar craving was satisfied and cigarettes extinguished, the men considered satisfying some of their other needs.

My father's mining experiences in Colorado and his need for sugar and tobacco, are the basis for my next commentary.

In our home town of The Plains, Virginia, (pop. 800) during the 1930's, the country's first advertising genius made his home. Mix Dancer was from Chicago, but he had a farm in Virginia near us.

In 1932, he created the Lone Ranger program for radio and found as its sponsor the Ralston Company. In the early thirties, the Lone Ranger was the most popular radio program in America and Ralston cereal the best known American breakfast food. Who can forget the exciting theme music that introduced that program, the Overture to William Tell?

Mix Dancer created the first nationwide advertising program on radio. It was Mix Dancer, my father insisted, who was the first human to understand mass media advertising.

The other day I was watching Italian television in my hotel room. Satellite reception permitted me to flick through more than thirty programs in half as many languages. The display impressed me. American products were being advertised with American music in the background as prelude to American feature movies to be shown with dubbed-in Italian voices on many stations. The influence of America was manifest.

The thought occurred to me that American consumer products have a remarkable opportunity — a head start on their competitors. Technical advances in television, I know, have been around a while, but the potential for worldwide marketing via satellite is truly in its infancy.

Simultaneous with satellite developments, political changes have expanded this marketing extravaganza. In Eastern Europe, the fall of communism permits the intrusion of foreign products in a score of nations with a population of 500 million consumers. In Asia, there is an awakening of a similar nature. The people of Thailand, Malaysia, South Korea, Singapore and perhaps China are reaching out for consumer benefits that the people of the Western world have long enjoyed. Their populations are far greater than ours.

Meanwhile, installed residential television in these backward nations grows rapidly. It is another craving.

The appetite for consumer products that have long been denied in less developed nations, but enjoyed in our country, will soon be satisfied. For the first time, underprivileged foreigners will be exposed to Madison Avenue methods of mass merchandising that will sharpen their appetites for products like chocolate, coffee and cigarettes. It is especially remarkable that just as these huge international markets are opening to exploitation, mass marketing techniques to reach them have become possible, as well, through satellite television. The importance of these simultaneous developments cannot be overemphasized. They suggest a rapid increase for brand name product sales worldwide; a trend, with a very long life expectancy.

Procter & Gamble, Philip Morris, Coca-Cola, and others will benefit. Each of them have vast resources for mass media advertising and a wide array of desirable, if not essential, consumer products to sell to people who crave them. Think about it. We are witnessing an important turning point with America in the lead for a change.

If Mix Dancer were alive today, he'd be in the middle of this international business.

"What do you think, Tonto?"

"You right, Kimosaby."

GOLDAMNIT

My dad was a successful mining engineer and someone quite unlike me. Naturally I wanted to involve myself in a successful venture that might mimic his successes.

In 1972 I was working on a mining project in New York that I thought would be the crowning achievement of my career. I thought Dad would be impressed. If memory serves, I lost most of my money and my self-respect during this strenuous period, while Alan Abelson in Barron's Weekly castigated me in the process. Now, twenty years later, my wounds are healed, and I am ready to reveal all.

The description of events which follows suggests an irrational behavior on my part that deserves an introductory note of explanation.

My dream was the dream of most ambitious corporate types, a passion among officers, directors and serious investors alike;

I wanted to take control of a business. There is an abiding faith amongst businessmen that they can run a business better than the person in charge. In my case it was an unshakable faith. Furthermore, I didn't care what business it was so long as I could direct it.

This dream became an *idée fixe* after my studies in the mid-sixties about gold and the South African gold market. I wanted to run a gold mine.

In the early 1970's, the opportunity to take control of a company listed on the American Stock Exchange presented itself. I guess you might say I seized it. Through a series of corporate maneuverings and S.E.C. filings, with five fellow shareholders, we won control of the Board of Directors of Valley Metallurgical Corporation. It was a company with almost no active business with a significant stash of excess cash, about seven million dollars.

One of our directors was a Canadian, a charming promoter who lived by his wits and occasional finder's fees. My Canadian director had an interest in a Canadian gold mining property that had recently been reequipped. The promoters had run out of funds before the reequipping or modernizing was completed and the property was available. The Chibex Mine in Chibougamau, Canada seemed the perfect vehicle, the ideal investment for Valley Metallurgical. My other directors agreed. While gold's price was rising and U.S. stock markets falling, we emptied the Company's coffers and purchased the Chibex mine in Chibougamau, Province of Quebec.

The Chibex mine required only a few more pieces of equipment added to the cyanide gold dissolving circuit and the mine could be in full production. Even before the delivery of these final items, we were blasting and crushing ore 250 feet below the earth's surface. It was early summer, 1974.

It happened that Canada was then in the throes of a serious labor dispute. The nation's truckers and railroad employees were on strike. As a consequence, no equipment deliveries were made to the Chibex mine for several weeks. Two hundred eighty employees assembled at the site were fed and housed everyday waiting for the equipment to arrive. There they sat in the summer's warmth, reading magazines, drawing their salaries.

While we survived this costly delay, another more sinister

development emerged. The newly installed cyanide circuit did not operate efficiently. When installed, it delivered less than 80 percent of the gold from the crushed ore, rather than the 90 percent that was expected.

Notwithstanding this setback, we produced more than twenty thousand ounces of gold during this fateful period, albeit at a substantial loss. The cost of installing a new circuit, as well as the delay such action entailed, was life threatening to our operation.

While these events in early winter were eating away at my waning confidence, a third and final event brought about our complete financial collapse.

The Canadian Government informed us we had inadvertently violated the Foreign Investment Review Act, a law designed to restrict takeover bids by foreigners. The Review Commission, in Montreal, denied our heart rending request for an exception. It was apparently better that two hundred eighty Canadian miners lose their jobs in mid winter than American investors should own the Chibex Mine. When the news arrived, I was heartsick. The mine was closed, the men dismissed and the place dismantled. Within a week, the 250 foot shafts filled with underground water.

Shortly thereafter, Alan Abelson in Barron's Weekly administered the coup de grace. In an article, a part of which accompanies this chapter, he held my directors and me up to scorn. It was my first exposure to publicity, and it was not exactly what I had in mind.

Even as the ink was drying on Alan's comments in Barron's, the price of gold was coursing upwards from $90 per ounce towards $800. That hurt worst of all.

As I look back now on the Chibex affair, I suppose I have learned a little. I no longer need to control a business.

BARRON'S SEPTEMBER 1, 1975 — PAGE 19
"UP AND DOWN WALL STREET"

"...Okay, so how did Valley Metallurgical come to buy into a Canadian gold mine? Well, as we piece the curious sequence together, the apparent inspiration was that of Murray Sinclair. Mr. Sinclair, a Canadian gentleman of venturesome cast, has been a director of Valley since '69. So has Richard E. McConnell, who became president and chief executive officer in '73, and William M. Weaver, Jr. a partner in the brokerage house of Alex Brown & Sons. In '69, too, John L. Burns, who formerly occupied top-brass positions with RCA and Cities Service, joined the board. This June, however, Mr. Burns resigned as both a director and chairman.

"In any event, one sunny day—July 25, 1974, to be exact—Valley Mining, a wholly-owned subsidiary of Valley Metallurgical, signed an agreement with Chibex Ltd., which calls Quebec home. Under the pact, Valley advanced $7.3 million to Chibex to bring a gold mine into production. In return, Valley became the proud owner of one-third of the gold mine. Subsequently, it sold 14.7% of its interest in the project for $1.1 million. Which is why Valley ended up writing off $6 million-plus, instead of $7 million-plus.

"Part of that 14.7% stake was sold to Canadian Memorial Services, which as its name implies, is in a grave line of work. Canadian Memorial Services also is 22% owned by Murray Sinclair, the self-same director of Valley. Mr. Sinclair has earned $150,000 as a finder's fee for putting Valley and Chibex together. In addition, a loan of $320,000 he had extended to Chibex was repaid out of the funds advanced by Valley to Chibex...

"...Even so, the joint mining venture went sour less than a year after it was launched. How come? According to Valley Metallurgical's 10-K: The grade of ore mined was approximately the originally calculated grade, and the tonnage of ore processed through the newly constructed ore processing mill substantially reached design specifications of 750 tons of ore per day in April

1975.'' However — and here's the rub, according to the company —'' the amount of gold recovered after processing the ore through the mill did not meet the design specifications of the mill which called for 90% recovery of gold.

''This failure, it seems, could have been corrected by a further investment of perhaps $750,000. After assaying the pros and cons of sinking this additional sum in the venture, Valley decided the cons outweighed the pros. So instead of committing another $750,000, it chose to write off $6.4 million...

TAPE WORM

One day my father announced to me he had been losing weight and attributed his failing condition to a tapeworm. It turns out a country doctor in Middleburg, Virginia told him he was smoking too much. Dad gave up smoking and gained weight rapidly.

That brief flicker in my memory causes me to reflect on another more widespread, self induced illness that I suspect is not so easily cured.

The Eastern European bloc of Communist nations reminds me of a tape worm that is about to be ingested by the industrialized nations of the free world.

As more and more information is gathered from these countries, revelations about their economic conditions become increasingly appalling. A population of 450 million people in Russian and Eastern Europe are living in poverty and are suddenly crying out for

Western aid. The thought that these are the same nations that were meant to pose a serious military threat to the free world seems almost ludicrous today, considering the serious shortages of food and bare essentials evident throughout communist Europe.

The burden their newborn freedom will place on the free world is certainly not military, but appears much more likely to be a financial drain on Western resources far greater than military outlays might have required.

We may be entering a period totally unlike the one we saw a short time ago. The possibility that the "Gang of Seven," the industrialized nations, will try to rescue Eastern Europe from economic disaster may be a mission greater, by far, than the Marshall Plan following World War II.

An economic scenario calling for peaceful coexistence, a lowering of defense budgets in conjunction with moderating inflation, may no longer be possible. Instead, we may soon see inflation rekindled as loan packages are arranged to save our brothers of Eastern Europe. New strains will be placed on the economies of the West, and especially ours. After all we are a nation of Europeans.

East Germany, the wealthiest of all Comecon nations has called for an immediate $9 billion loan from West Germany to East Germany. The Deutsche Bank President has forecast West German aid of $300 to $500 billion to East Germany in the next ten years. Of course, no one today has a number to suggest as a rescue package for all the others, but the figure must certainly be huge, or as my kids say, humongous.

It is probable the industrialized Gang of Seven will attempt to restore a semblance of economic order in Eastern Europe through Government loans and subsidies. If so, they will have ingested a tape worm that will keep their economic prospects and ours thin for a long time to come.

INDIGESTION

The downfall of Communism in Eastern Europe suggests to most people a great and long awaited victory, but to me it represents as well, a terrible cost that will have to be shouldered by western democracies. I envision a tapeworm slowly eating the economic substance of the more fortunate nations for years to come, as West helps East rebuild these broken economies.

It wouldn't surprise me if the West Germans were already having second thoughts about their hasty union with East Germany. Politically, it may still have strong appeal, but economically it has become rather unpleasant. Not only are the East Germans in need of current necessities, which the West Germans must finance, but they also need an entirely new industrial base for the future. Not to worry, there are only a few million East Germans and a lot of marks in West Germany.

The West German affection for their woebegone relatives may be misplaced. The costs of friendship may offset the rewards originally hoped for. Only time will tell.

The Israeli program to extend a similar hand of friendship to the Russian Jews is an even more burdensome act of generosity. Economic life in Israel is already strained.

Little Israel — a nation of 3 million hardened freedom fighters has offered refuge to another million or so Russian Jews. Three hundred thousand have already arrived in haste from Russia in 1990. A similar number may show in 1991. The press reports from Shamir's government suggest the great pleasure that all Israelis feel at their arrival. That may be, it's early yet; but it is a bit more brotherly love than some of the Israelis I know think advisable.

Whereas the early settlers of Israel were young, eager, and oftentimes well educated or trained, the new influx of immigrants from Russia is comprised of former communists who have not been trained to be industrious. They are not the hardened Puritans who settled Massachusetts or the frontier people who moved west of the Mississippi. These are a softer breed, unprepared for a life of continued hardship in a very hot climate. The West Bank is no place like home.

Although Mr. Shamir's generosity may be well meant, it's highly improbable Israel can afford, let alone benefit, from the influx of so many impoverished people. Moreover, the cost of this ill-advised generosity will most surely be a problem for the United States as well. In addition, this influx is occurring at a time when tourist traffic to the Holy Land, the largest industry by far in Israel, has come to a near halt, while military expenditures continue rising. West Germany might be able to muddle through; but Israel has little chance even with our help. And all this at a time, when the world is over-sensitized to Palestinian questions. The whole plan is ill-timed, to say the least.

Now before you take aim with a scud missile at my innocent observation, don't shoot — I have a solution.

I suggest that every Russian Jew who aspires to a free life and new freedom in Israel be told the truth, the whole truth and nothing but. The truth is that life in Israel is going to be tough, hot, and dangerous. So tell them to come prepared; bring light clothes and a gas mask! Maybe they'll stay home.

Do you remember a line from the Walrus and the Carpenter? "...thick and fast they came at last, and more and more and more, all scrambling through the frolicking waves and landing on the shore..." Do you remember what happened to those oysters that scrambled through the frolicking waves and landed on the shore?...

402 EAST 42ND STREET

A friend of mine in the publishing business looked over some of my recent comments and decided he was not interested in them for one of his publications. He said they weren't long enough to make an article or a column and they had rather limited readership. He wondered if my children enjoyed them. He doubted it. He invited me to lengthen my observations and expand my subject base, and then he might reconsider.

I had a short epithet for him that I mumbled when we parted, but he did cause me to think a bit. I have decided I cannot lengthen these articles even if I wanted to. The subjects I write about are not subjects on which I have great knowledge. I've never been to Iraq or Russia; I'm surely no economist; and I know less about the stock market than some good brokers. It's quite enough if I catch your attention for a moment with one of my passing thoughts. Now here's a subject I know absolutely nothing about.

In 46 years, membership in the United Nations has grown from 51 to 149. Most of this growth resulted from the breakup of the British Empire and to a lesser degree from the creation of new nations from German, French, and Italian possessions.

Today it appears another wave of expansion for the U.N. is in prospect. The collapse of Communist Europe may create many more fledgling nations from the Baltic to the Black Sea. There are more than a dozen potential U.N. members that may arise from the strong nationalist movement that is threatening the Union of Soviet Republics and the satellite Communist world. Yugoslavia may show up with more candidates. I cannot recall a time when the demand for independence was heard in so many areas from so many curious ethnic cultures.

The Eastern bloc, that once voted at the U.N. as a single communist voice, may now vote as twelve or fifteen independent voices. The balance of power may be greatly altered as each of these new countries expresses its opinion. Nations like Japan, Germany, Korea, and some of the OPEC members may grow in stature as money lending members, while Russia may exhibit a softer, impecunious voice. The security council may thus have to be reconstituted.

It is probable that more than a few of these new nations will obtain independence only after a costly civil war. Democracy will have a difficult time asserting itself in these countries where its benefits are so little understood and its tenets so seldom practiced. It goes without saying that most of the newcomers will be poor and in need of assistance like those predecessor members that arrived after World War II from darkest Africa.

The new United Nations may make the older one seem like a cage of nightingales in comparison, when some of the newly elected members start singing off key.

In New York City cacophony is a familiar song.

THE TOWER OF BABOIL

The recent Iraqi face-off with the Western World is not the first time the Muslim minority has been in conflict with non-Muslim nations for economic reasons.

The Crusades of the 14th Century were fought for economic reasons to stop Arab forces from the interdiction of the spice trade. It's hard to believe but a peppercorn was a medium of exchange in those days with a value that sometimes exceeded the value of human life.

Today it's *déjà vu* all over again. It was oil, not spices that set the world's teeth on edge this time.

Mohammed, the Prophet, was born six hundred years after the death of Christ. In the Koran, Mohammed is said to have revered the words of Jesus. The Muslim religion was not a bar, or obstruction but an extension of Christian ideals. But all that was before economic forces had their way. The Crusades put the kibosh on Muslim friendship. A handful of Arab tribesman raided the camel caravans with spices from Java to steal these essential food preservatives bound for Europe. You know what happened then?Richard the Lion Hearted returned from the Crusades to England in defeat.

A few months ago a similar fracas was initiated by another handful of camel drivers. This time the attempted theft was oil, the petroleum fields of Kuwait, not the fragrant oils and spices of Java. In the old days, spices were needed to keep our food from spoiling; today oil is needed to keep our cars from stalling.

We may be in luck this time, unlike the hopeless days of King Richard, when earlier campaigns from England failed to break the strangle hold of Muslim domination. This time the fragile alliance of OPEC may be shattered.

If you ask me, Saddam Hussein has unintentionally started the final chapter of the economic grasp of OPEC. By his attack on Kuwait he became public enemy No. 1. He caused other OPEC nations to increase their oil production to make up for the shortfall from Kuwait and Iraq. In a few months producers met the challenge and satisfied world demand. Hussein's production was no longer needed.

No matter how you view his holy war, Hussein has probably done the world of car owners a big favor. He has thrown the future of a pernicious cartel in doubt. He has unofficially been dropped from OPEC. His re-entry may be subtly resisted if not denied. No one needs him. So why let him back in?

Imagine the impact on world oil prices when Saddam asks for his fair share of OPEC oil sales. His products will be contraband bought only by infidels. Every barrel of Iraqi oil sold will push world markets down to lower and lower levels.

The prophecy of the Old Testament will have been fulfilled again. The unholy alliance of OPEC will be dispersed like the tribes of Israel at the Tower of Baboil.

An Open Letter to Saddam Hussein
Bahgdhad, Iraq

Dear Mr. President

I have been thinking about you.

The frequent overthrow of one leader by another in various countries of the World has led me to consider writing a book of instruction for aspiring despots. It is a subject that must be of interest to you. I was going to call it a "Tyrant's Handbook."

I am still working on one of the last chapters that I hope you'll like.

A TYRANT'S HANDBOOK
Chapter 10
How to Commit Suicide

It's a rare tyrant who doesn't fear his ultimate downfall from an assassin's bullet. As a result, he may indeed consider suicide as an alternative. Here are some helpful hints for the ruler who had everything and wants an assured final exit.

Step 1: Overrun a defenseless nation with a surprise military attack.

Step 2: Remove all this neighbor's cash and deposit it to your account; declare the neighboring country non-existent.

Step 3: Seize by force all foreign embassy personnel in the defeated nation's capitol and remove them to your country's capitol; call them "involuntary guests."

Step 4: Declare your actions a holy war against Jews and Christians.

Step 5: Invite a Western leader and former Nazi to your country, and as a gesture of human kindness, release his nation's embassy personnel formerly held hostage.

Step 6: Run the U.N. blockade of ships sent to arrest your piracy on the high seas.

Step 7: Then declare war on all U.N. members except Libya and threaten the use of mustard gas.

These seven simple steps will assure an aspiring national leader like yourself, a prompt departure from this mortal state and a place in everlasting infamy.

Sincerely,

Since no one in his right mind would follow these instructions, I'm sure my handbook will not have wide appeal. It's too silly.

But just imagine the gyrations in the world's stock markets if someone tried it and lived.

OILYBABA

Lawyers are often measuring both sides of a controversy before rendering legal opinion. For amusement I decided to hear an opposing view of a recent dispute that at first blush, seemed to have only one point of view. The Iraq crisis and the Gulf War was the case in point. President Bush argued the United States' case extremely well, I thought. But I have now read an Iraqi closing argument.

The interview was by an Arab reporter with whom Saddam Hussein seemed at ease. It was a pretty good presentation of the Iraqi point of view, but I cannot remember to save myself where I read it. Here it is now from my notes almost verbatim.

President Hussein:

"Our country is like any other landlocked nation that wishes to export its goods to foreign markets. We need a seaport. We are tired of pumping our oil by pipeline across our neighbors' lands with no assurance it will reach its final destination."

"I seized Kuwait, a tiny plot of land no larger than Israel, after consultation with the American Ambassador. I needed a seaport for the economic health of my country. I offered every citizen of Kuwait Iraqi citizenship. Within a few weeks only a few had not accepted my generous offer."

"Is this the act of an aggressor? Not in my mind. The United States took possession of Hawaii without outside complaint. The British did that sort of thing for years and got away with it. Kuwait was a British protectorate when I was growing up. Israel seized the West Bank from Arab residents by force; but people now consider me an aggressor. I don't get it. Some nerve."

"Kuwait, you remember, was the only important member of OPEC that violated its quotas and held the price of oil down through overproduction. What greater example of greed can you recall? So I went in and put an end to their destructive efforts."

"By my act of daring and statesmanship, this selfish practice of Kuwait treachery was ended; the price of oil returned to acceptable levels. At least twenty oil producing countries like England benefitted from my courage. Don't forget, Kuwait was no nation, it never was; no usable land, no army, no population, no industry. It was created by British imperialists before oil was discovered there."

"We now have given back what really was ours; returned Kuwait to its sovereign status; handed it back to the Amir and his cabal so that a few greedy men can continue to receive uncountable wealth."

"My people and the people of true Muslim faith everywhere show respect for me, their leader, they know I acted in their interest. Can President Bush say the same of his people? Can he claim support for his acts as I can?"

"Look what has happened since we gave in to Mr. Bush and offered to withdraw troops from Kuwait. Cowards have returned who escaped our arrival. They have returned from Saudi Arabia. The great oil wealth of Kuwait is now back in the hand's of a few citizens who never worked a day in their lives; who would not fight for their country, who hired foreigners as their servants while robbing the world of a great natural resource? They don't work even now. They let their oil fields burn. No dear brother, Kuwait was always rightfully ours, and someday the Royal family will have to work for a living or be deposed. Call a free election in Kuwait today, and see if I am wrong."

"I'll let you in on a well guarded secret, dear brother, before I go. It's an example of Saddam's cleverness."

"I have six doubles in my employ, six men who look exactly like me. That's why I appear so often in public, in the streets or with my troops. My enemies cannot tell which of the six men is the real Saddam. To kill me they will have to kill six other men before they are sure, and that will be a very tough assignment. It will never happen. So if you read of my assassination, don't be too sure... I shall live."

"I sleep perhaps better than President Bush; my people are behind me, my cause is just and I serve my God. Allah be praised. Good night."

That's all I remember of this remarkable interview, but I was impressed.

Naturally, I haven't changed my mind about which side I am on, but I am intrigued with Saddam's questions about Kuwait's future and the future of its oil. I don't think I would have handed it back to the ruling Kuwaiti's if the decision had been up to me. My suggestion would have been to give it to the United Nations as a U.N. protectorate. That way we could use Kuwaiti oil production to maintain adequate supplies for world consumers. Isn't that better than dividing $18 billion of annual revenue amongst Oilybaba and his forty thieves?

THE MUDS OF ABANO

My dad once remarked that senior citizens were tiresome. All they talked about was their health. He found his health of interest, but thought everyone else's totally boring.

The following thoughts have some boring material in them about old people, but happily no medical advice; they concern the health activities in Abano, Italy and my visit there. I wrote it in order to introduce to you a petit denouncement, which is the surprising part at the end of this essay. So please read this piece in its entirety.

The mineralized soils of north western Italy, near the Dolomite Mountains, contain a gray mud that is a healing miracle for arthritis sufferers. The town of Abano is the center of this health community which has been a popular spa since the time of the Roman Empire. Nero had his own private bath in Abano.

I went there last Fall and stayed at the Hotel Trieste and Victoria. The main entrance was spacious and comfortable, while the back door gave way to rows of hot tubs. My fifth floor room overlooked these steaming vats.

I was interviewed by the resident physician the afternoon I arrived. He spoke no English, so my medical examination took place in idiomatic French. The doctor looked Eastern European to me and I expected him to appear like Bela Lugosi in evening attire for dinner.

After breakfast the next day I entered a tiny tiled room with a single cot, stall shower, and small tub. At the head of the cot was a 50 kilo mound of steaming slime. The room smelled like an intensive care unit for gangrene.

A plump matron beckoned me to the center of the room and pulled the curtain behind us. She tested the mud's heat with her elbow. I couldn't help wondering if her elbow was as sensitive to heat as some of the more sensitive areas of my body. She ordered me to disrobe in sign language that a lesser gibbon would comprehend.

I stripped and stretched face up on my narrow bed. She smeared recycled slime over me, and then covered my body in canvas and heavy blankets. In 20 minutes, I was removed from my casserole and hosed down while standing bare. I was next immersed in a bubbling tub for a final cleansing phase.

It was all over in 45 minutes. I had had my first mud bath, and was released. Outdoors, I found a large heated pool for an hour swim. The area smelled of Clorox.

So it went for two weeks with only Sunday set aside for rest. The treatments were miraculous, and I now feel much better. I know you are pleased.

I discovered something while I was there, however, that I should mention. It may not be so pleasing.

The hotel is part of a consortium of hotels in the area known as OPAC (Organization for the Pricing of Arthritic Cures). The purpose of OPAC is to monitor the distribution of the muds of Abano, and to set fair prices. Nothing pernicious in OPAC's efforts to conserve the use of their healing muds, is intended, but a few patrons I talked to believe the creation of OPAC may have been just an excuse to keep prices high.

Someday the hotel owners may face serious arguments from millions of arthritis sufferers who are denied the healing treatments of Abano, simply because they cannot afford them. If the owners aren't careful, a serious conflict might suddenly break out. The short Mud War of Northern Italy might make a tough exam question for future students. They might get it confused with the one in the Persian Gulf.

THE MIKADO

"What a Pretty Mess In A Month or Less"

I remember a time when I envied everything Merrill Lynch represented. The intelligent ease with which its analysts surveyed the world economic scene was nothing less than awesome.

But things have changed; my envy has ebbed.

With all due respect, I think we are watching a transmogrification of financial institutions.

The bankruptcy of Drexel Burnham, the $200 million write off of Merrill Lynch, and the massive capital deficiency of Shearson Lehman, are today symptomatic losses occurring in Wall Street. The bloated investment community continues to downsize. Layoffs are occurring at nearly all major firms as margins have narrowed dramatically. The major sources of profit for Wall Street have been reduced through lower commission rates, higher overhead, and increased competition. At the same time, the business of financing companies, especially the leveraged buy-out craze, has all but come to a halt.

Program trading and volume discounts for large institutional accounts have driven the disadvantaged public from the market so trading activity is almost all institutional and highly competitive.

The number of Wall Street employees has fallen from a high of 260,000 in 1987 to a recent level of 200,000. Drexel Burnham's enrollment dropped 4,500 in a single day. If this trend continues, many stocks may go unnoticed for lack of a motivated Wall Street salesman to pitch the story or a research analyst to report its higher worth. As Ed McMahon likes to say, "no salesman will call." Maybe something like this is in store for stocks.

Lower valuations for most stocks could follow just as occurred after the "paper blizzard" of the early 1970's and the earlier collapse of Wall Street in 1973-4. Hayden Stone, Dupont, Goodbody & Co. and Walston were significant firms in the Wall Street community then. With most of the identical problems that firms face today — lower commissions, higher overhead, and increased competition — these firms failed. They were replaced to some extent by Japanese firms such as Nomura Securities, Daiwa, Yamaichi, and Nikko. Now they are in trouble.

In view of the scandals lately in Japan on the Nikkei Stock Exchange, I think we should call the present New York Stock Exchange dilemma the Mikado and blame it on the Japanese.

WINDEXING

Believe it or not, there's a widely accepted investment practice on Wall Street today involving one fourth of the value of our nation's pension assets. Not many people know about it. It's called indexing. It's a system by which pension sponsors invest their funds in a static pool or index of stocks that mirrors the movement of the popular market averages. It saves on commissions and management fees.

This idea, which gained wide popularity in the eighties, is based on the observation that most investment managers cannot outperform the stock market. As indexing gained wider and wider acceptance, this embarrassing observation became a self-fulfilling reality, a prophecy; the more pension funds indexed, the higher the index rose to make room for new commitments. Consequently, indexing was a winning formula.

I believe that is now changing. It's my guess that the late comers to indexing are about to be cleaned. So please humor me just this once, I have renamed this Wall Street fad WINDEXING.

Since the start of the stock market recovery in 1975, a new investment phenomenon has taken place in the institutional market. I am speaking of indexing. It has replaced an earlier and equally powerful investment style called growth stock investing. The increased popularity of indexing in the seventies and eighties supplanted the growth stock craze that held institutional sway in the fifties and sixties.

Let me recollect for you the history of these two developments and reflect on the probable outcome for the current trend setter.

In the early fifties, it was T. Rowe Price of Baltimore, Maryland who first espoused the growth stock doctrine to the institutional market. He observed that some companies' earnings grew faster than others, and that they should, therefore, be accorded higher multiples. Current yield, under his philosophy, could be ignored.

This "remarkable" new concept of neglecting yield for earnings growth became accepted doctrine for the large trust companies and institutional investors in the sixties, until no self-respecting investment manager could do without it.

By 1972, the growth stock concept had been transmogrified to become the "nifty fifty." In its final stages of evolution, growth stock multiples were taken beyond reasonable levels of value before the 1973-74 bear market produced the sharp and painful reversals that this concept so richly deserved.

Indexing has no single author to whom the investment name can be ascribed like T. Rowe Price. It is an invention of the banks whose investment records, in the seventies, were so poor they reverted to indexing to save embarrassment and further erosion of their business. The scheme actually worked. The idea of investing in a static index of stocks rather than a managed portfolio was an idea whose time had come and sold well. Yet stand by. Like a chain letter, indexing needs more and more adherents to work otherwise it will take its place alongside junk bond investing. In fact, it is already happening; let me explain why.

A stock index is usually composed of a few large selected companies that represent our nation's principal commercial efforts; an aggregation of giant old line firms that are America's major industries.

These companies, General Electric, IBM, Kodak, U.S. Steel, General Motors, and Alcoa are the fine old firms that are found in every index fund. They have an extremely large asset base. They are the last dinosaurs.

Once upon a time, they had far better balance sheets, they sold at book value. That was before indexing. Today many of them have impaired equity bases that sell at twice book value.

They are companies with long histories of hidden deep-rooted problems: things like seeping waste, unfunded medical expenses, potential product liabilities. These companies are like the unimpeachable growth stock values once found in portfolios that the bank and insurance industries revered. Today, these old companies have been finding write-offs not increased profits, to reflect to their shareholders.

Moreover, some of these indexed giants are not what they appear to be anymore. U.S. Steel is partially an oil company, not a giant steel company; General Electric is a broadcaster, stockbroker, finance house, as well as a manufacturer; General Motors is Electronic Data System and Hughes Aircraft; Kodak is Sterling Drug. Many of the index components are really conglomerates. As such, they have uncertain centers of assured earnings.

One of the best run conglomerates with the fastest rate of earnings growth in the sixties and seventies was Gulf and Western Corporation. It rarely sold above ten times earnings despite its phenomenal growth record. There was and still is a prejudice against conglomerates. Why should G.E. sell at a premium multiple. It is a conglomerate. One has only to compare the spread in value between G.E. and the smaller companies in America to see what has taken place since the advent of indexing. The smaller companies are far better values.

In my mind, indexing was an idea whose time came and has now went.

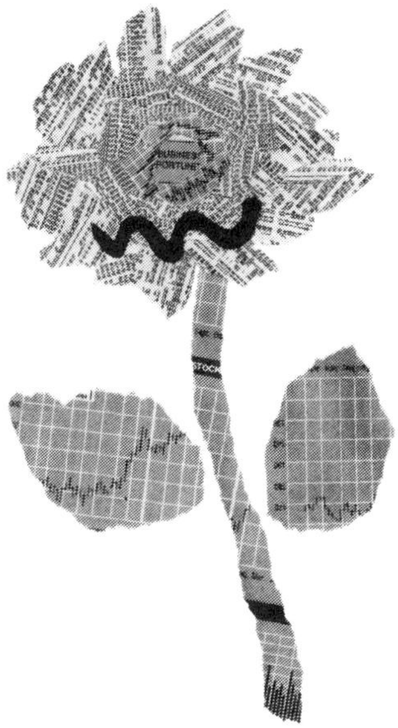

MEASURING THE MARIGOLDS

A survey of stock market experts appeared in Barron's recently. The author claims to have canvassed one hundred sixty top investors to get their opinion. His failure to seek mine is understandable; it's very difficult to remember all the best players. I, for one, was surprised to find there were so many.

Nevertheless, I decided to add my thoughts on the market's outlook to the Barron's article, despite the fact that no one asked me. Forecasting is actually what I do best.

The first thing I look for in making a forecast of market behavior is the "frenzy factor." I look for extremes. Whenever, the prevailing view is excited and optimistic, the market is vulnerable, and whenever there is a pall of negative sentiment in evidence, the market has probably found a bottom. There, that's all there is to it.

Today, sentiment appears to be evenly divided, if Barron's article is an accurate measure. There is no strong consensus either way.

So I am comforted in believing that the market's reaction to forthcoming news will be restrained. I am also assured that the preponderance of the economic news will be bad.

And for those of you who are still reading my prognostications or any others for that matter, I'll let you fill in the last word.

I think the stock market is on its way ______.

That wasn't so hard, was it?

Years ago, Danny Kaye popularized a nursery rhyme I remember:

"Inchworm, inchworm
Measuring the Marigolds
You and your arithmetic
How beautiful you are."

I am beginning to think we spend too much time gauging the market's direction; trying to guess the future like inchworms. It's a waste of time. Wall Street has become a colony of inchworms.

MIRRORS

Would you like to know how we got our first client?

I remember the day I visited Tom Murphy at his offices at Capitol Cities Broadcasting to make our first presentation. Boy, was it brief! As usual, Tom's desk was clean, and he greeted me with warmth.

"Tom," I asked, "do you like limericks?"

Maybe he said, "what's yours?"

I answered quickly. "Mirror, mirror on the wall, what's the cheapest stock of all?"

He paused, thought a moment, then with slight impatience, he said "Dick, I'll bite; what?"

"I think Capital Cities Broadcasting is the cheapest stock of all, Tom, and I think I can prove it."

I then showed him the figures we were using to evaluate stocks. Tom looked at them for several minutes; he was interested. He called John Shuff, his financial vice president to join us.

"John let's put a little money in Dick's firm and watch closely," he said, "I think he's got something."

That was the start of our firm, our first client, Capitol Cities Broadcasting, nearly fifteen years ago. It was also the low of that company's stock price which has risen twenty times in value since then.

My story is merely prelude to a present market practice I want to explore with you. Today many people try to guage market direction. They use economic forecasts, charts and an astounding array of assembled figures to forecast the stock market. But they are never right consistently, only occasionally. A long while ago, my firm abandoned that practice and focused its attention on individual stocks, exclusively. Nevertheless, I continue to dabble in market forecasts. Here's an example of my present state of confusion.

I have attached a chart from the Federal Reserve Board that purports to trace the make-up of buyers and sellers of U.S. stocks for the past ten years. There are five major categories of participants listed and I assume this is a complete list. No important category of buyer or seller has been left out.

Tracing the buyers and sellers of U.S. stocks for the past 10 years, to me, shows a menacing trend. And if the source of information were anything but the Federal Reserve Board, I would be suspicious of the figures. In fact, I am anyway.

The first and most obvious observation from these charts is the public's retreat from the stock market during the greatest bull market ever. Individuals, for a myriad of reasons have largely abandoned stocks for other things. As usual the public has been wrong.

Next, and more recently, the new liquidators of our stock market have been the private pension funds. Maybe most of them are now overfunded and would prefer to move to the sidelines; or cash in. For whatever reason, they have had a change of heart and they are a current source of selling pressure.

Finally, the foreigners and the public pension funds that once stepped up to fill the void left by the individual sellers, have lost their recent taste for stocks. I wouldn't be surprised to see the foreigners, especially the Japanese, become net sellers.

So, if everybody who used to buy stocks in the United States is selling them, what's holding the market up?

Another glance at our chart, the left hand column, must be the answer. After all, for every seller there must be a buyer, and the Federal Reserve shows us in Column 1, the corporations themselves are buying or tendering for the stocks others are selling.

Despite the fact that corporate balance sheets deteriorated to the lowest level in memory in 1990-1, and corporate earnings appeared to be in a downtrend, the corporations continued buying their stocks.

But who will be buying stocks and keeping the Dow Jones Average at 3000 in the nineties?

Don't ask your broker, he doesn't know. His industry lost millions in 1990 and while his lot is improving, it is not because of stock exchange volume.

The Germans and the Japanese have their hands full these days. Don't look to them.

Not the private or public pension funds, I can testify to that.

Maybe its all those people in the underground economy that don't tell Mr. Greenspan what they are up to; the people who launder their money in Miami. Or could it be that Eastern Europe has untold wealth seeking employment in our free economy? Maybe.

I have a final guess. I'll hold back for now. It's your turn. But if you think of someone I've missed, I'd appreciate a call. We should compare notes.

STOCK MARKET SUPPLY AND DEMAND*
($BILLIONS)

	Net Corporate Acquisition of Stocks	Foreign Investor Acquisition of Stocks	Direct Public Acquisition of Stocks & Equity Mutual Funds	Private Pension Fund Acquisition of Stocks	Public Pension Funds Acquisition of Stocks
1980	$ -15.0	$ 5.4	$ -12.8	$ 16.4	$ 5.3
1981	8.8	4.8	-43.0	17.3	7.1
1982	-11.1	3.3	-15.4	12.3	6.0
1983	-27.1	6.0	-9.2	4.5	20.0
1984	66.3	-1.3	-69.7	5.4	7.3
1985	68.0	4.3	-93.1	-9.0	28.6
1986	69.6	17.2	-101.4	-8.5	23.1
1987	55.1	15.6	-71.8	-27.8	26.4
1988	118.1	-0.5	-131.8	-20.3	25.9
1989	116.7	7.7	-102.9	-20.4	8.7

Equities As % of Financial Assets:	Foreign	Public	Private Funds	Public Funds
Range 1968-1989:	16.2 - 38.4%	19.0 - 43.4%	49.6 - 71.4%	12.1 - 38.8%
12/31/89:	23.0%	19.6%	57.3%	38.8%

* A negative number signifies a net seller of stocks.
A positive number signifies of net buyer of stocks.

Source: Federal Reserve Board

SOUND SHORE MANAGEMENT, INC.

WAITING FOR THE GNU

I now pen my answer to a mystery I uncovered in a note I called "Mirrors". I do this sort of thing frequently.

I raised the question of the stock markets' continued strength at the start of this decade in the face of strong selling by most categories of investors. The same chart I attached then, I now attach reflecting the dilemma I raised. But this time, I have updated the figures.

Current figures reveal the answer to my question.

The general public has been large buyers of equity mutual funds. The figures were not wrong, they just weren't up to date. Individuals, after a prolonged absence of 25 years have been buying, in the first six months of 1991 $15 billion in funds versus $1 billion in net acquisitions a year earlier. At long last John Q. Public is back.

This renewed interest on the part of the private citizens in stocks may be foreboding.

It reminds me of a French documentary film I saw years ago about the life cycle of the African gnu.

When someone asks what I think of the stock market, I am reminded of that French documentary film. It describes the incredible migratory annual trek of the great herds of African gnus; a journey of more than a thousand miles. The gnu is a durable small animal that serves as haute cuisine to most of the carnivores of Africa. The hyena, lion, and winged carrion-eaters of African nature follow these herds on their annual trip north, selecting the weak ones for their insatiable appetites.

On the last day of their terrible journey to green pastures and fresh water, across the endless Serengeti Desert, the gnus reach the Mara River ravaged by thirst and hunger. As they approach the water, they smell the river's odor even before they see it.

In panic and thirst, a million exhausted animals break into a stampede, creating a cloud of dust as they race to the river, signaling their arrival. For more than two miles, the young gnus approach the river's bank faster than their parents. They unhesitatingly plunge into the dark quenching waters.

The first of them are greeted by scores of hungry awakened crocodiles. Only after these prehistoric reptiles have gorged themselves on the young gnus is it safe for the older ones and remaining calves to drink. The treacherous 1,000 mile journey is at last at end, and the cycle of life in the gnu community is over for another season.

The cycle of most, if not all bull markets, ends after a final frenzy, in which the public is a major participant. The public is presumably the young unwary member of the investing herd. In the past several years it has not participated in this rising market. Only recently does it now thirst for its profits.

Consider for a moment whether the investment cycle has made its full turn; be alert like awakened crocodiles. And wait patiently for the gnu; or is he already here?

STOCK MARKET SUPPLY AND DEMAND*
($BILLIONS)

	Net Corporate Acquisition of Stocks	Foreign Investor Acquisition of Stocks	Direct Public Acquisition of Stocks & Equity Mutual Funds	Private Pension Fund Acquisition of Stocks	Public Pension Funds Acquisition of Stocks
1980	$ -15.0	$ 5.4	$ -12.8	$ 16.4	$ 5.3
1981	8.8	4.8	-43.0	17.3	7.1
1982	-6.6	3.3	-15.4	12.3	6.0
1983	-23.6	6.0	-9.2	4.5	20.0
1984	70.8	-1.3	-69.7	5.4	7.3
1985	70.9	4.3	-93.1	-9.0	28.6
1986	73.4	17.2	-101.4	-8.5	23.1
1987	60.9	15.6	-71.8	-27.8	26.4
1988	126.2	-0.5	-131.8	-20.3	25.9
1989	121.7	6.6	-111.8	-17.9	23.7
1990	56.9	-16.0	-30.5	-14.2	6.3
1991 - 1	15.1	10.9	12.6	-11.2	5.0

Equities As % of Financial Assets:	Foreign	Public	Private Funds	Public Funds
Range 1968-1990:	16.3 - 38.4%	17.0 - 43.4%	49.6 - 71.4%	12.1 - 40.8%
12/31/90:	18.9%	17.0%	58.3%	37.4%

* A negative number signifies a net seller of stocks.
A positive number signifies of net buyer of stocks.

Source: Federal Reserve Board

SOUND SHORE MANAGEMENT, INC.

COUNTERFEITING

My father gave me a short book about inflation for my fifteenth birthday. I remember the book's title, all right, but nothing else. Nevertheless, early in life, I was exposed to the evils of inflation. I now accept his view that any government that fosters inflation by printing money is no better than a coffle of cunning counterfeiters.

Here are some of my current observations about printing money and what I think will soon happen as our Government goes deeper and deeper in debt.

If you think the American public's recent interest in equity funds is a frenzied buying trend, then take a look at the renewed interest shown by our citizens in government bond funds. It is a zest that hasn't been seen since World War II bond rallies. Investors who lost confidence in the banks and S&Ls recently have withdrawn their deposits and sought refuge in Government bonds. It's one of the reasons Federal auctions have been successful. The public has been taking an ever increasing, if temporary interest in Governments.

There has also been demand from the Social Security Trust Fund. The Trust's receipts are running way ahead of dispursements. So the Fund has been a very large buyer. As retirement benefits mount, and dispursements rise, the Fund will soon discontinue buying government paper. The Social Security payments will then be larger than receipts; much larger.

Then there are the foreign buyers; the ones who see the present rising value of the dollar as an added inducement to their ownership of U.S. Bonds. They not only get interest on their money, they get the increased purchasing power of the dollar when they convert back to their national currency. How long this trend will continue I couldn't say but it could easily go the other way as it did a year or so ago. The foreigners could decide to back away from U.S. obligations if the dollar sags again.

Thus it appears that most of the present buyers of Government bonds have had a nonrecurring interest in the gilt edged market. Their purchases could evaporate without notice at any time.

The recession in 1991 reduced demand for capital in the business community; corporations didn't borrow. They didn't need the money for growth. If the recession is over, as some seem to think, then corporations may return to the capital markets, increase their borrowings and compete head to head with the Federal government at the auction tables. The recession, which created a window of opportunity for the Federal government to sell bonds at favorable rates, may now be closing.

So I suspect that the appetite for Government obligations recently has been inflated and largely from nonrecurring sources. For different reasons the major buyers won't be around for the giant auctions that are coming. Sales of bonds in the future may be more difficult; the business of counterfeiting may not be so easy any more. It is a unique period in our history, when the act of printing money is becoming a hazardous occupation almost like basement counterfeiting.

Douse the lights! I think I hear someone coming.

WAMPUM

American history has a bit of trivia in it I like.

It seems the peltry trade in the American Colonies was a thriving business during the seventeenth century; the settlers and the Indians swapped buck skins for whiskey. I don't remember the going rate for beaver skins, but the rate of exchange for deer hides was five bucks for one gallon of liquor. Deer skin britches were all the rage in seventeenth century Europe. The rate of exchange for deerskins, five "bucks" per gallon, was how the dollar bill got its name. It came to be known as a "buck."

I should stop with this tidbit, but I cannot resist going on to tell you what this historical fragment suggests to me.

For a nation to establish an acceptable currency as a widely respected medium of exchange is a difficult and time consuming responsibility. It takes years. Most countries have currencies that are acceptable only inside their borders. Their foreign commerce is largely barter, like deerskins for booze. Such nations operate at a decided disadvantage. The convenience of paying cash in world trade with your own country's money is a privilege still limited to only a handful of developed nations.

In recent years, the volume of trading in these "acceptable" and "hard" currencies has risen dramatically. Today approximately $300 billion in currency value is traded daily by banks. This number dwarfs the value of world trade. Furthermore, the annual currency trading value of $90 trillion is many times the value of all "acceptable" currencies in circulation. It is a very recent trading phenomena that has little or no relationship to the financing needs of international trade.

The money center banks today have found trading currencies, a new source of income, aided in part by super fast data transmission systems. They are running the world's largest crap game, buying and selling currencies, with stakes higher than any gambling play ever devised. Miraculously, so far, no major losses have been reported.

Yet, to me, there is something threatening in this daily trafficking. It's an unregulated sport run by exuberant youngsters at their trading computers; the same inventive players who gave us junk bonds and program trading. It is a very highspeed practice, the offspring of a computer society gone mad.

While this buck swapping business has been growing, the "buck" has been falling: fifty percent in value against a basket of other "acceptable" or "hard" currencies. Of course, that's not the sole reason for this fall. But a fifty percent devaluation in so short a time is, to me, serious business, like a major military defeat. No kidding. It's a loss of face that casts doubt on our financial strength and our future security. It is our neighbors' evaluation of our politics, our people, and our prospects. While the dollar's value has come back recently this does not allay my reason for concern. I still worry about kids with computers at major money center banks.

If we don't stop squandering our financial reputation and return to financial responsibility, we may someday find our only trading partners no better than Indians in buckskin britches.

So save your wampum, I say, just in case the money center banks take another header.

8 ROCKLEDGE ROAD

I rarely receive inquiries from friends asking my opinion, so it really pleases me when this occurs. My biggest surprise came last month when a friend called to say he was considering buying a waterfront home in Rye, New York. It was something he had wanted all his life, and he wanted my opinion.

He then proceeded to recite for me his analysis of the economic outlook for real estate and the probable impact of the recession on residential values in the New York City area. As he talked, I concluded that his mind was made up so I decided to go along. I did not mention some of my depressing thoughts and forebodings. Deep down, I thought his decision might prove regrettable, because we were, I thought, at the top of an economic cycle; and in real estate, like cattle or tomatoes, that can be a bad time to buy.

Before you call me a spoil sport or pessimist, however, let me explain.

In 1922, Mother and Dad bought a large stone house in Bronxville, New York on eight acres of land. It cost $80,000.

My father had been successful in Wall Street as an investment banker; his mining background gave his small firm an expertise in mining securities that other larger firms lacked. By the time he was forty and a father of four, Dad was financially independent.

Late in 1930 on a routine visit to an insurance company for a medical exam, he discovered he was not eligible for life insurance. He was working too hard, apparently, and his heartbeat reflected the hectic pace of his business life. He decided to retire and do what he had always wanted to do, but could never afford. He bought a farm in Virginia. He and mother moved to Middleburg, Virginia in 1932. There were ten of us by then, my parents, five children, a German governess, and two very large dogs.

Meanwhile, the house in Bronxville was put up for sale, the summer of 1932 — the bottom of an economic cycle. For two years, despite sales efforts, there was no serious bid for this home. Finally, in 1935, father gave the property to a boys school and took a tax deduction of $50,000. The IRS, one year later, disallowed the amount deducted and later settled for half that figure.

I wanted to tell my story to my friend and suggest he hold up on his purchase until he had at least sold the house he was living in. But that's probably not what he wanted to hear. Besides, his wife and mother-in-law were excited about redoing the living room.

MUNICIPAL BOMBS

I attended a wedding reception in New York for a young stockbroker and his bride recently. The newlyweds announced to me with pride, they were moving into an apartment on York Avenue on the 34th Floor.

At the reception, my friend was feeling expansive and asked my opinion about the future of New York. We were interrupted, mercifully, and I didn't have a chance to reply to his inquiry, but I thought about it.

The next day I wrote down my thoughts.

Back in 1973, the health of New York City and its financial community was drawn in question. New York City was (and may still be) the center of world finance; many money center banks and brokerage offices are headquartered in Manhattan.

During the City's economic crisis in 1973, Felix Rowatyn headed a committee to restructure New York's finances. By a series of migraine maneuvers, he persuaded the policemen, the firemen, and the teachers to use their billion dollar pension assets to finance the City's return to solvency. Recently, he warned of another city crisis; but this time he said, the pension assets of City employees won't be available, they have been spent.

As I think about it, things are mighty different now than they were when Felix was in charge, and, perhaps a good deal worse.

We now have an AIDS epidemic. We didn't know what it was in 1973. Today every hospital is losing money largely because of AIDS. If the 30% growth rate of the disease continues, AIDS patients will occupy all hospital beds now available in New York City by 2000 A.D.

Drug use has expanded. A far more destructive drug, crack, is a new part of this epidemic. Crack didn't exist in the 70's. It is cheaper and produces the addiction more rapidly.

The banking industry is now in trouble. It wasn't then. To find a street without a bank on the corner then was difficult. To see a corner with a bank today and you see a vacant store front.

The penal colonies, like Riker's Island, are overcrowded. Places designed for 800 inmates rarely house less than 1,300 these days. They smell bad.

The crime rate is worse than it ever was; the residents are afraid to be on the streets at night. Even a nice guy like Bill Cosby is licensed to carry a hand gun.

The Federal Government is in no position to help out this time. I can't remember if it helped out last time, but I seem to remember President Ford's friendly advice to the City's mayor: "Drop dead." Today you may hear a similar Republican rejection.

The homeless are a new and growing source of shame, and a problem for the new city government.

While real estate markets fell sharply last time, this time we have a national real estate crisis to insure a sharper correction.

Lastly, technology permits those who don't want to stay to leave the city. Things like fax machines, lap top computers, and networking computer systems permit whole divisions of corporations to leave town.

Have I left something out? Probably, but I think it's clear. The outlook seems worse than it was in 1973. Good luck Mayor.

I called my young broker friend at work and sold some more municipals. I never mentioned my pessimistic thoughts to him because I didn't have the heart. He was too happy with my market order and the commission he made that day. I wanted to suggest he quit while he was behind, but he had already hung up. His wife was holding on the other line.

THE INFLATION FIGHTER

I have a friend in Westhampton Beach who is manager of the largest department store chain on Long Island. During the recent Gulf War he told my wife and me to buy two new pool umbrellas to replace our old ones and just store them until next summer.

"They are made of petroleum-based plastic" he confided, "and with the price of oil sky rocketing, they will be much more expensive next year."

Not since radio station WINS in New York dropped its hourly "inflation fighter" program in 1981 have I heard anything so disturbing. For ten years now, I have seen prices stabilize, interest rates moderate, and the chances for peace improve. And in a single weekend instance of cocktail party chatter about pool umbrellas, it all ended for me.

As we all know, inflation is not a problem until inflation psychology takes hold. Only when people spend their money in anticipation of rising prices is inflation a real threat. I might also add that my wife is by nature frugal. She never acts on impulse. Yet last weekend she paid $400 for two plastic umbrellas she didn't need and put them, unopened, in the garage. I was cross at first, but on further consideration, I now think she may be right. I suspect inflation really is a threat.

We may be going back to President Johnson's era of "guns and butter" economics of spending much more than we take in and borrowing the diffference. This time we're not so well prepared either. Our debt loads are much higher, our deficits much wider. To make matters worse, once again, the U.S. has no economic plan to correct its spending habits: no financial goals, no goal line.

Think about it.

MELTING SNOW

My father was always opposed to debt except in cases of emergency. His early unpleasant experience with borrowing probably influenced this attitude his entire adult life.

In 1904, he borrowed funds from his aunt to attend college in New York. The crash of 1907 arrived, the start of his senior year. It placed financial hardship on everyone. Dad's father lost everything; his mother took a job in the town library, and on the day of his graduation from Columbia, his aunt asked for repayment of the loan. She had suffered economic hardships too. My father was desperate.

He left New York and found a job that summer in a lead mine in Colorado. He worked two full shifts underground each day. He was able to help his parents and at the same time pay off the debt to his aunt in the space of only two years.

Often he reminded me of these early experiences with pride. He said his first job taught him "the advantages of poverty." It is no wonder he believed in hard work and the avoidance of debt. It was his credo.

My attitudes are influenced by these recollections and are awakened by disquieting current events. Let me explain.

I have always enjoyed books on early American history. I was interested in the controversy that arose over the payment of Federal debt after the American Revolution. This controversy cast Alexander Hamilton and Thomas Jefferson in opposing roles, the former arguing for the honoring of the Continental Paper and Jefferson opposing this solution. U.S. debt was in default and speculators including Congressmen and elected officials, had purchased much of the debt at a deep discount. Jefferson suspected friends of Hamilton. It was our nation's first insider trading scandal. Hamilton prevailed and Congress authorized payment of Federal and State debts over a period of several years. By the beginning of Jefferson's second term in office, all government debt has been repaid.

This incident in history of insider trading is an interesting coincidence. The size of the post Revolutionary debt weighing on the three million American inhabitants in 1790 was similar to the per capita debt with which this nation's population is currently burdened. If the earlier debt is adjusted to an annual 3 percent inflation rate for the two hundred intervening years, then per capita debt then and now are roughly equal; a burden of $48,000 for every man, woman, and child.

But that's where the coincidence ends.

In the late 18th Century, debt was abhorred; debtor's prison the sad fate for anyone who could not pay. Today debt is encouraged. Creditors rights now are less favorable to the creditor and more lenient to the debtor. The Revolutionary debt was incurred in defense of liberty; today debt is incurred in pursuit of pleasure. While the prevailing view in 1790 was to pay off all debts; the current view is to add to them.

For the past few years, total debt in the U.S. has been rising nearly one trillion dollars annually. That's an amount equal to the external debt of all underdeveloped nations—each year.

This plight reminds me of a true story.

A friend of mine was sent to do a pictorial essay on the Missouri River for Life Magazine. The winter snows had been especially heavy and most observers expected the spring thaw would bring a big flood and severe damage down much of the Missouri, despite five giant dams built along this waterway to protect against such an emergency.

Snow has a nasty characteristic — it acts as a sponge and absorbs much of its own water as it melts. Only when it is in the final stages of dissolving does snow suddenly release all of its accumulated water. The final result, on a warm spring day, can be devastating. It was for the Missouri River one spring day many years ago.

Metaphorically speaking, spring floods on the Missouri may have little apparent relationship to our current thirteen trillion dollars of total debt. But I see a parallel.

I see total debt as the winter's accumulated snowfall. I view the coming of spring as inevitable, as inevitable as an economic cycle. The five dams on the Missouri River designed to inhibit floods are, like Federal laws, designed to mitigate sharp downturns; Unemployment Compensation, Medicare, Federal Deposit Insurance, Social Security, and Federal Reserve Authority are all examples of laws designed to block economic calamities. There is also the perverted phenomena that is found in humans and snow crystals; a capacity to at first ignore and then overreact to change.

In this contrived way, I view the future course of economic events as a probable flood brought on by melting snow.

No wonder Dad didn't like debt.

PHARAOH'S DREAM

Genesis 41

While I remain upset about increasing U.S. debt loads, I detect no such concern from my friends. Silence from my children and pals is not reassuring. My partners in Connecticut last winter were winking at each other in a patronizing way. They thought I was spending too much time in the hot Florida sun. Other comments that I overlooked were even less flattering.

I thought I'd rephrase my observations a bit to see if I could jump start someone's interest.

The 1980's were, from my point of view, one of the most profligate periods of U.S. economic history. Without threat of invasion or economic collapse, the U.S. Government, American corporations, and the American consumer all added to existing debt loads at an alarming rate. About $9 trillion of net new debt was added in ten years, an amount far greater than the cost of World War II; inflation adjusted.

To put it another way, if each dollar in $9 trillion were paid off in a single minute, our debt would have a maturity of 16 million years. I should wait so long.

Even so, not all these debt commitments of the '80's should be characterized as wasteful or foolish. Not like blowing up cities or shooting people. After all, U.S. employment went up, corporate profits rose, the stock market quadrupled, communism in Eastern Europe collapsed. In addition, the downward thrust of the economic cycle was postponed and the cost of rising inflation slowed its advance. Not a bad return on $9 trillion you might say.

"So what's the point? What are you trying to tell me?"

"The point is," I answered, becoming somewhat annoyed and having no idea what I was going to say next, "the 90's are here; today is the tomorrow I told you I was worried about yesterday; and the subject of too much debt raises serious questions for me!" I think it's a subject worth considering.

So if I don't hear from someone pretty soon, I'll assume no one needs to worry; I may as well doze off.

I hope I don't have that bad dream again about Joseph and the Pharaoh, (Genesis 41). Pleasant dreams. ZZZZZZZZ

THE ROUTINEERS

Someone named Huston Smith wrote a book in 1986 called THE RELIGIONS OF MAN. I am halfway through this readable volume and have already found guidance in it; not for my soul unfortunately, although that may come later. Let me quote from page 62:

"At the bottom of the social scale is a class of routineers whose time sense is so short that they cannot be counted on to forego... present pleasures for future rewards. These poor souls are relegated in the Hindu caste system to the lowest levels."

Well I'll be. I never knew that one of the great religions of the world had such strong words to say against our spendthrift society. The way I read it, our Congress is made up almost entirely of Hindu "routineers." If the U.S. population were living in Indian today, the Hindu caste system would relegate us to the lowest levels.

As you might guess, these sacreligious outbursts are by way of introduction to my next thought.

During the Iraqi face-off in the Persian Gulf with Western nations, the price of oil rose and I of course feared the reignition of inflation. That's because wars are inflationary (see attached chart). If war in Iraq had become extended an inflationary surge would have followed. But the incendiary ambitions of Saddam Hussein were defused. The result was that deflationary forces started to work again.

This sudden reversal in economic conditions may surprise many people who have become more or less adjusted to inflation and to the constant upward pressure on prices. We have come to consider inflation an integral part of our life; we expect it, some of us welcome it, many of us plan for it.

This attitude in turn has led us to spend more than we should, borrow more than we should, and forego future rewards for present spending pleasures, like Hindu "routineers." Our borrowing habits are a reflection of this spendthrift behavior. It may be an imbedded way of life. Inflation is the root cause.

In recession's wake (such as the one that appeared briefly in 1991), falling prices and higher unemployment prevailed. Oil paintings sold for less, so too real estate, commodities, furs, and toys. In fact, it was difficult to think of a cost that was not falling except the cost of government and medical bills. Debt liquidation was also in progress. This was the most telltale sign of deflation. But the condition seemed to me temporary even though prices went down, and may still be drifting.

Anyone who believes that deflation is permanent may be forgetting the growing Federal deficit. It is the countervailing force that will reverse deflation's progress. For 1991, and maybe 1992, deflation appears in the ascendency. But, to me, the trend is reversible.

Inflation is alive and well, living with unprecedented popular support at 1600 Pennsylvania Ave.

Debt marches on.

Sound Shore Management, Inc.

Effect of Wars on U.S. Consumer Prices

Smoothed 10 Year Moving Average

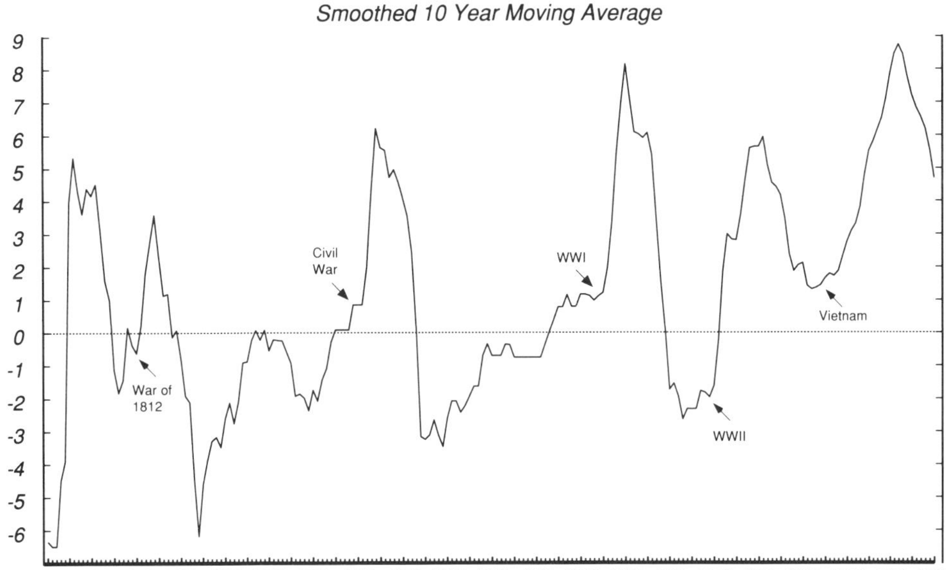

Consumer Price Index *Year to Year Percentage Change, 10 Year Moving Average* *Last Observation 1990 P*

1990 Preliminary through May
Source: Bureau of Labor Statistics

THAT SINKING FEELING

The basis for my increasing concern regarding the U.S. economy, is our nation's growing debt load; not just the Federal Government's as well. Debt has been expanding in the United States at an astounding rate, $700,000,000,000 dollars per year at last count. With this ever increasing debt has come heavier debt service that lessens the chances for economic growth. We have to make payments of interest and principal on thirteen trillion dollars ($13,000,000,000,000) of debt before we can pay for essentials. Debt service is a prior claim on everything, even food.

One reason our profligacy of past years has been acceptable on the world's stage of lenders has been our relatively high interest rates. Until 1991, rates on U.S. Governments were more attractive than those available in Japan and Germany. But things have changed. After adjustment for inflation, Germany's rates are now higher than ours; Japan's are as well.

Another reason our borrowing behavior has been tolerated and lenders ready and willing to absorb increasing debt issuance has been our economic prosperity. Corporate profits were rising in the '80's and prosperity seemed assured. This too has changed. Corporate profits are heading down, the first downturn in eight years. My opinion is that there will be slower growth or none at all in 1992 and beyond.

In addition, the quality of debt has fallen. We have seen downgrading of many classifications of bonds as well as a number of disquieting bankruptcies and defaults.

Things have sure enough changed, not for ever but for now.

Nevertheless, there is always reason to hope. The demise of Communist aggression has so lessened the chances of war that major industrial nations can now focus on peace. The world's military budgets can be reduced; a peace dividend declared. But this won't come soon. First things first.

Pessimistic views are always popular, widely held, and presumably fully discounted in the market place. Most investors build large cash reserves that reflect the same concern. Therefore there is no need to worry.

I, for one, am not impressed with this point of view. There are times when even nerds share the correct majority view — pessimistic though it may be.

Popular opinion aboard the Titanic after it struck an iceberg, was correctly pessimistic even among the strong swimmers who earlier shared the well advertised view that the Titanic was unsinkable.

Despite our country's size and strength, our growing debt load is reason enough to be concerned even if everyone knows about it. It gives me a sinking feeling.

FOOLISH LENDING

Please bear with me. I was just beginning to accept the idea of a mild recession and soft economic landing when the Near East War materialized. Before I could adjust to this surprising development it ended. Higher Federal defense costs were endured but only briefly; then the real problems resurfaced, the ones brought on by foolish lending. But for me there were new aspects to this old problem.

The U.S. savings and loan crisis is the most obvious example of big losses that arise when the Federal Government enters the financial guarantee business. Recently acknowledged Federal losses from student loans, while not nearly so large, are still another embarrassing example of this unfortunate tendency. The same goes for the mistaken commitments at the Small Business Administration. Percentage wise the losses in SBA are the worst of all. Then, there is the foreboding suggestion that the very largest Government guarantee program may be in trouble; the Federal Deposit Insurance Cooperation.

Directly and indirectly the U.S. is guarantor of many more bad deals than was ever thought possible a short while ago. Yet there seems no strong movement or present effort of our Government to call a halt.

Like the Federal Government, the large banks have amassed a poor lending record too, led on, in part, by the Federal guarantee programs. The underdeveloped nations are in arrears on their debts to our banks. Very large commercial and industrial real estate loans are in trouble coast to coast. Tanker, farm, oil, and leverage buyout commitments are a pockmarked record of recent bank lending. These are the reported or known trouble spots. Others may soon surface.

It's no wonder most banks are now redrawing and restricting their lending procedures. A voluntary, if not involuntary, credit crunch may be near at hand.

Liberal lending habits by banks and the Government in the 80's were largely responsible for the growth in our economy that we enjoyed then, and now have to pay for. It is unlikely we shall enjoy a repetition of such growth and credit ease in the near future, at least so far as the banks are concerned.

If the Federal Government tightens its many guarantee programs, the possibility of severe credit restraints seems probable.

Maybe lending for spending is ending.

FIREFLIES

I used to run through fields at dusk gathering fireflies. When I had gathered twenty or more, I would run back to my parents and show them. I often went off to bed to watch my fireflies glow in a jar.

As I write now, I am still chasing fireflies to put in my jar.

Here are more of them from my imaginary mason jar. I'll punch holes in the lid, in case they smell a little.

My concern for some time has been the increasing debt load that our nation is amassing. Corporate, personal, and government debt has quadrupled in the ten years from 1980-1990 from three trillion to thirteen trillion dollars.

In addition, since the collapse of communism in Eastern Europe, Western nations appear poised to spend vast sums rebuilding the broken economies of Europe while draining their own strength.

This was the condition I found the U.S. financial community in 1990, and I was concerned. As time progressed, I found other reasons for increasing concern.

Massive debt loads were not our only transgression. There remained a vast network of guarantees of the banks, the insurance companies, and the Federal and State governments that had not been addressed; these were obligations, albeit contingent, that had not been considered by me until recently.

Never mind Saddam Hussein, the Japanese market collapse or the rising Federal deficit, there were those hidden problems that began to surface.

There were also corporate obligations for retiring employees for health coverage that were not funded. And public responsibilities for old age benefits and health care promised, that had not been budgeted.

The massive contingent liabilities which look less and less contingent as time goes by are the hidden threats to economic balance that make me worry—never mind our current debt loads.

These are the fireflies, I keep. They smell a bit.

SKIDMARKS

I have been writing about the stock market environment and the growing debt problem, the plight of the brokerage industry, and the lack of fiscal morality like there was no good news, no improving trends.

All my messages have been tinged with a negative bias. However, I expect to have a change of heart someday although not real soon. I thought I would tell you why, before you dropped off, since I live in fear that my pessimism may be like the story of the renowned-but-now-forgotten economist who predicted five of the last three recessions.

If I could only eliminate my preconditioned pessimism, I might now begin to see the unraveling of the excesses of the past. The number of changes that have already taken place in 1990-91 have been positively remarkable and they seem to be largely constructive.

Let me list a few.

The Nation's foremost leaders in the banking industry, under Government pressure, have become bill collectors. Lending policies are now very restrictive. The dollar has gained strongly.

The Resolution Trust, charged with managing the assets of bankrupt thrifts is in the midst of a gigantic forced sale. Real estate prices are under pressure. It is a painful but corrective movement.

The junk bond market has lost its following; Drexel Burnham is bankrupt, the participants like Mike Milken, Charles Keating, Fred Carr, and other "Barbarians" face law suits, indictments, and jail. No matter what the outcome of these suits, Congress has already restricted program trading with a "collar." Ivan Boesky has paid his debt to society.

The corrective process is well along, and it is no longer in its early stages.

Future economic events will probably add strength to these early corrective forces. Municipal bond ratings will continue to be downgraded, as state governments, especially in the Northeast, face economic reality and raise taxes. In addition, these same governments have already enacted legislation to restrict takeovers, proxy battles, and green mail. Stock market raiders are out looking for work.

Markets previously closed to U.S. producers will open in Japan and Eastern Europe as trade restrictions are lifted. South Africa may be readmitted to the world economic community.

The Brazilian and Polish governments have announced draconian anti-inflation measures. The Russians are experimenting with capitalism.

The Japanese market decline, has proven a valuable and sobering experience. This too is part of the corrective process.

Finally, high society in New York has announced it will opt for less glitz. Ivana Trump has time for her children, her ex-husband has given up gambolling.

Perhaps, most important of all, the rise in overall debt (except Federal debt) is slowing, and that's some turnaround. We seem to have hit the brakes.

Before you rush out to rejoice with your friendly stockbroker, I suggest you watch the road ahead carefully. Anti-lock brakes haven't yet been invented to handle high speed economic matters.

A LITTLE HEDONISM

As an antidote to my notes on the outlook for the U.S. economy and to assure other more sanguine authors equal time for the presentation of their views, I am submitting excerpts from a book entitled "Megatrends 2000."* Optimism abounds in the very opening sentence:

"In the decade of the 1990's, the world is entering a period of economic prosperity."

I excerpt other sentences that support the author's basis for optimism:

P. 24 "There will be no energy crisis to impede the 1990's global boom. Quite simply, the world is using less energy while producing more."

P 26 "The growing worldwide competition to lower taxes... will also help expand the global economy of the 1990's."

P. 29 "It has begun to dawn on people everywhere that war is now an obsolete way of solving problems, certainly among developed countries."

P. 33 "In reality the domestic deficit is not out of line with what it had been for the last forty years..."

P. 36 "If all the numbers are tallied, the United States has no trade deficit with Japan or the rest of the world."

P. 38 "It is a mystery to me," says Milton Friedman, "why it is regarded as a sign of Japanese strength and U.S. weakness that the Japanese find it more attractive to invest in the U.S. than in Japan. Surely it is precisely the reverse — a sign of U.S. strength and Japanese weakness."

P. 40 "In the 1990's, the United States will have a younger population than either of its major competitors — Europe and Japan."

P. 93 "The odd couple, Mikhail Gorbachev and Margaret Thatcher: each dismantling the welfare state."

There's lots more. Purchase this book soon, and read it for yourself. It's worth it, even if you find the statistics a bit overwhelming.

I found the book slightly more comforting than the advice of my old friend from Akron, Ohio. He wrote to me last month and advised me to forget the Old Testament and "Pharaoh's Dream" and try a little Hedonism.

That may be all right for him to say; he's not married and he's 84 years old. I still have my children and grandchildren to think about.

RUNNING ON EMPTY

I want to go out of this life a proper prophet like Nostradamus, Moses, or Nebuchadnezzar.

My lifelong ambition is to be the very first man to call the exact date of the end of the economic world, preferably to a large and attentive, relatively well informed audience. So I have written this book. That's what I am up to. You are that well-informed audience I have been searching for all this time.

I haven't got it all worked out just yet; the official timetable, that is, but I can give you my E.T.E.D. (Expected Time of Economic Departure), more or less on the button.

Let me cover the highlights of my analysis while I have your riveted attention, and I may catch you up later on the final disastrous figures.

President Bush, January 1991, in his State of the Union address announced his budget for the fiscal year. It was an unremarkable report suggesting Government expenditures of $1.4 trillion and a probable deficit in excess of $300 billion, not including the cost of the Iraqi War. No one in authority knew then what that warlike item would finally tally, so rather than hazard a guess, government officials just left it out altogether from the budget estimate.

A private group in Washington said our cost for the short spat with Saddam Hussein was $200 billion. I don't know that firm personally and since the war is now ended we can assume it was probably a cheapy; so let's forget it.

Six months later budget director Richard Darman hazarded another guess in June 1991. He suggested a $338 billion deficit in fiscal '91 and a probable $358 billion deficit in the following year.

Only a few days later he stated that there might have to be an upward revision in his red ink estimate because Government receipts were running $130 billion below estimates.

Secretary Baker's offer to replace civilian losses suffered by Iraqis after the war has been largely forgotten; but every high official seems to be overseas making promises.

Stock market reaction to George Bush's straight forward address in the winter of 1991 and to Darman's that followed, contained no alarming reverberations for shareholders in U.S. stock markets. Apparently investors accepted the ballooning deficit matter-of-factly. Earlier estimates of the probable deficit were simply dead wrong. So wrong, in fact, that in a less solemn period they would be considered ludicrous. Thus, present prospects of a Government deficit of $400 billion, must be considered conservative.

For those of my readers who have stayed with me while I have harped on this subject — increasing debt loads and probable calamity — I now wish to reaffirm that view before you leave. I view the fourfold increase in ambient debt from $3 to $13 trillion these past few years as ominous, even scary like the Texas Chain Saw Massacres. I trust I have made myself plain on that point.

Now, here I am, all alone with federal and state debt burdens hurtling higher and higher, and U.S. stock markets rising almost in lock step. I'm wondering about the precepts of Professor Graham's first year class in economics which I attended at Princeton University. I must have been dozing.

In this heady atmosphere of military triumphs, diplomatic achievements and optimistic forecasts, I am at a loss. It's like a town with only one television station, there's no other viewpoint, and it is extremely optimistic and every one is watching but me.

The tricky question for me that needs answering now is not if these debts will cause long lasting damage, but when the presence and commanding influence of possible insolvency on a national basis will invade the investment mind and be felt in Wall Street.

That is the question that I pose now and which I shall answer for you. Pay attention!

I pick May 7th, 1992 as the exact date when values fail; the day of ruin, the beginning of the end of economic life as you and I know it.

It's a day, shortly after April 15, when most citizens have paid their Federal taxes: A Thursday when all taxpayers, have had a painful few days to consider their new bank statements and found them to be running on empty.

No question about it anymore, in my mind, Tuesday, May 7th, 1992 is our day of financial infamy.

So if you will pardon me, I have some last minute chores to attend to. Adieu.

One last comment before I go. On the odd chance my forecast turns out to be premature, I'll rework the figures for you and write another book.

IN GOLD WE TRUST

At least once a month I visit a small brokerage office in New York and talk to the various partners about the stock market. The firm's members are a loosely wrapped bunch who have widely divergent views.

I asked a young partner on my last visit to tell me what stocks he was considering that day for investment. Without hesitation he said gold shares. He removed a chart from one of his file drawers and showed it to me. What his graph appeared to reflect was a ten-year history of sideways movements in the price of gold. The chart meant nothing to me, while it appeared to impart far more lucid meaning to him.

I thanked the young man for his provocative suggestion and hurried out of his office in time to lunch with his father. Needless to say, my careful questioning of his father over soup produced none of the suggested potential for gold I had heard from his son, so I dropped the matter.

I have recently reflected further about gold and have come to the unsolicited opinion that the young partner was dead wrong; he's got it backwards. Gold shares, as well as gold prices, will go down, not up and for good reason. In fact, I reckon that within a year gold prices will retreat $100/ounce while gold shares will do worse.

If you wish to know why, just send a check payable to me for $300, and a self-addressed stamped envelope, and I shall send you my compelling analysis. Please note that your $300 payment will fully cover my purchase of one ounce of gold someday. Allow five weeks for processing and handling of your order.

No wait! On second thought, forget it; don't leave! I was only kidding. Just keep reading and enjoy my opinion without charge.

A closely guarded secret in Russia today is the location and quantity of gold held by that Government. There are less than a handful of top people who have access to this information.

Whatever else you may suspect, there is a strong probability that this horde is quite vast and readily deliverable by clandestine order from a very few top Russia officials. These officials know the location of their stash. They may even be disgruntled ex-party members, disillusioned, and tempted to seek asylum from Russia with their valuable knowledge. Whatever else happens, Russia will be a desperate seller of gold in the future.

On the other hand, Iraq and Kuwait, which were once important buyers will probably be sellers from now on. The rebuilding of Iraq and Kuwait will drain their formidable reserves.

Future German purchases of gold may be reduced now that German interest rates have risen from 5 percent to 9 percent and while East Germany's economic needs are simultaneously approaching infinity.

Japan may also buy less gold since its interest rates have recently doubled and its economic growth has slowed.

Moreover, the international business community may not buy as much gold as it used to. As I mentioned in an earlier note (Wampum), world financial traders can trade currencies and hedge temporary risks in far greater amounts today than has ever been the case in gold markets. Inconvenience and risk of gold delivery are eliminated as well. In fact, trading in gold is decidedly more subdued today in part because of currency trading by money center banks for business clients.

By George, I cannot think of one new source of demand for gold that will take up the slack created by recent events. So, while supply remains constant (or rise with increased Russian sales), and demand loses its earlier strength, the price should fall. It's as simple as that — fewer buyers and perhaps a few desperate sellers. I'm surprised it hasn't happened already.

For a few years then, I suggest you avoid gold shares whose price earnings ratios are very high. The current strength of the dollar, like the motto on our American currency, suggests a better alternative for investment and a much better postulate of faith than the title of this piece implies.

If you are not currently an owner of gold shares, do not lightly discard this important thought — save it! For a year or so the $13.5

billion in value of North American gold shares will be ghastly investments. But, when you least expect it, inflation's forces will reemerge and gold stocks will respond to rising gold prices and improvements in earnings. At that time you may wish to reconsider your allegiance to the American dollar and its catchy slogan.

Incidentally, you may remember that the slogan "In God We Trust" was first inscribed on American currency in 1864. That was the year of our country's highest inflation rate since its founding.

AN AMERICAN TRAGEDY

If I were qualified to write my own American Tragedy as a sequel to Theodore Dreiser's great work, it would be about the last years of Thomas Jefferson at Monticello. Not that I know a great deal about Jefferson, but he was my father's hero; someone I heard about most of my life.

Dad believed Jefferson was a tragic figure. Of high birth and great wealth, Jefferson dominated the American stage in its formative years. As with all great men, he had a tragic flaw. He consistently spent more money than he received, and he borrowed to satisfy his appetite for beautiful possessions. In consequence, he died insolvent on July 4th, a half century after the date of his greatest achievement, the final drafting of the Declaration of Independence.

Jefferson was saved from total embarrassment by the Virginia

Legislature, which, at his request, permitted him to sell his assets at lottery. Virginia law at that time forbade gambling, but the legislature made an exception in the case of its former leader.

In past chapters, I have been droning on and on about the dangers of excessive debt, the dramatic increase of consumer, corporate, and government debt in America. I have wondered about the disastrous consequences of this development all by myself. I now find consumers, retrenching a bit, and corporations finding solace through bankruptcy protection. But the Federal Government shows no such signs of regret. Federal deficits continue coursing upwards at record levels, accelerating in part because of a minor recession, a small banking crisis and the end of a happy little Gulf war. Someone could almost congratulate our fiscal leaders. But not me! There is no evidence anywhere to suggest that the U.S. Government has found investment religion. Quite the contrary, the increasing support debt loads continue to receive from the American electorate encourages the politicians and makes things even worse. Mounting deficits are either accepted or ignored.

In my earlier chapter on the sudden growth of debt "Melting Snow," I was reminded of the controversy after the American Revolution in which Hamilton and Jefferson had opposing roles, the former arguing for the honoring of all Federal obligations and Jefferson instinctively opposing this solution. I sense that the present generation, like Jefferson, is not anxious to honor its debt.

In another letter "That Sinking Feeling", I noted the astounding rate of debt expansion during the Reagan presidency.

I stayed upset and expanded on my outrage in another chapter, and in another few wasted pages, called "Pharaoh's Dream," I appealed for some sign of agreement.

In the chapter "Foolish Lending," I blamed the S&L crisis on Federal Government guarantees just as my exhaustion reached vendetta proportions.

I rambled on, castigating a poor fellow in Westhampton Beach who suggested prices were about to rise; "The Inflation Fighter". I didn't disagree with the old gentlemen, but I disliked the loud voice in which he made his forecast at a cocktail party with women present.

I then settled down to a repetitive droning about the risks of increasing debt, "Fireflies," and threw in a criticism of accumulating municipal problems, "Municipal Bombs."

For those who were still reading, I continued with "Wampum," questioning the future acceptability of our currency in foreign markets.

I even forecast the day when our sins would find retribution and values would fail, economic life as we know it would end, "Running of Empty." I thought that this last effort would take care of things, and like Paul Revere, I could dismount. Are you kidding? I have been riding through a countryside of sound sleepers.

Ever optimistic, I now summon the memory of a great man, Thomas Jefferson and I ask if you see the similarity between his final years and the current spendthrift days of this nation?

I declare that we are about to rekindle inflation. We are about to reenter the years of "guns and butter." Higher prices will return.

So next, I shall ride again like Paul Revere on a faster steed and clamor to suggest what's coming; what most assuredly is in the offing and what corrective action we must take. Perhaps, just perhaps, by my daredevil ride, we can avoid the financial consequences of rekindled inflation.

THE THOMAS JEFFERSON AWARD

My father thought the Lewis and Clark Expedition and the Louisiana Purchase the greatest achievements of Jefferson's life.

"A good lawyer could have drafted the Declaration of Independence or founded a great university," said Dad, "but only an outstanding leader could have had the courage and foresight to invest in a vast unknown tract of wilderness with such benefit to his countrymen."

Dad made a donation of $10,000 to the University of Virginia in memory of Jefferson. He called it the Thomas Jefferson Award. The income from this gift is presented each year to a member of the University's teaching staff whose teachings most clearly reflect the teachings of Thomas Jefferson. That was in 1951.

Today, the Thomas Jefferson Award is the highest honor bestowed on an instructor at the University. It is awarded on Founder's

Day amid great fanfare and press coverage.

The financial impact of the gift, however, is no longer significant. Through attrition, the $500 annual award is only symbolic. Inflation has reduced the gift's purchasing power, to a decimal of its former worth.

It is the erosion in value of well-meaning donations that prompts these present comments. Oddly enough I am now party to the same error made forty years ago, by my father.

On October 31, 1991, the Harvey Mudd College in Claremont, California dedicated the Baker Chair in Biology. In honor of Harvey Mudd College's second president, an endowment of $1,000,000 donated by college trustees was presented. It's income supplements in perpetuity, the salary of a member of the biology teaching staff.

If history is any guide, the efforts of the donors will be miscarried. The income from this endowment, although adequate now, will be inadequate a few years hence to attract the teaching talent needed.

The reason for this failure will be the same as the reason for the financial failure of the Thomas Jefferson Award. Inflation will destroy the Baker Chair's value.

I think I know the reason for this failing; I think I know why we, as investors, aware of the dangers of inflation, do so little to avoid them.

Would you like me to explain? All right stand back a bit, I need room.

Most trustees charged with responsibility for investing money have two objectives: creating an adequate return for the life tenant and preserving the corpus for the remainderman. That's what the law mandates, so that's what they do. Nothing is said of purchasing power. No mention is made of inflation.

Magically, trustees seek a 5 percent annual return from the assets under supervision and simultaneously the preservation of the principal. It's the prudent thing to do, so long as they are not getting paid to do it.

Today investment committees invest 50 percent in bonds, the rest in common stocks. It's the prudent approach and a low risk posture.

Investors today think common stocks have been a hedge against inflation. They believe the Dow Jones Averages have kept up with the rising cost of living. That is a common conviction. But look again; it isn't so. Since 1966 the Dow has failed to keep pace with inflation, otherwise this index of stock values would be standing today at 4200, not 3000, this calculation includes the remarkable thrust of the bull market of the past 12 years. Bonds have suffered an even more severe fate in the same space of time. We simply do not realize how pernicious inflation has been, or even how its threat continues.

It is imperative we remember and remind ourselves that inflation is alive and well luxuriating, with unprecedented popular support, like I told you, at 1600 Pennsylvania Avenue.

EASY COME, EASY GO

My dad never discussed Thomas Jefferson's final years of insolvency, but he knew of his hero's financial failings. It was probably Jefferson's only weakness, which my dad ignored. This unfortunate mark on Jefferson's history reminds me how easily even great men dissipate their wealth.

I see no reason not to use Jefferson's tragic end to reveal my concern about other pockets of wealth that may disintegrate.

My father used to remark that a man spent twenty years of his life saving twenty thousand dollars and twenty minutes investing it. He often said that people don't seem to attach the same importance to making money as they do to investing it.

Most institutions run their money in a similarly relaxed manner. People do too. The mistakes are commonplace. Not surprisingly then, most investment programs are unsatisfactory.

Colleges, for example, appoint an investment committee from a voluntary list of its board of trustees who have no serious qualifications for appointment, except perhaps their innate desire to make some contribution to education. It's a hobby.

Committees meet infrequently to run the assets, sometimes six times a year. It's often difficult to get a quorum. Decisions, therefore, of one meeting are often not shared by absent members and are sometimes a minority view. There is rarely a strong consensus opinion except a prevailing attitude featuring "low risk" investing.

This is not the structural basis for superior investment results. It is a system that almost can't work even though it is applied frequently if not universally. Just for the moment, let me suggest perhaps a way to improve the structure.

1. Appoint a two or three man executive committee with investment experience to select the investment managers and oversee their work. Let them meet twenty times a year, maybe more.

2. Place responsibility for market timing on the investment managers; that is their responsibility. Do not let the executive committee become a market timer of the stock market's direction. That rarely works.
3. Appoint another subcommittee to deal with legal and procedural matters. These details, although important, often make up the greatest part of the full committee's agenda. Separate the two functions.
4. Invest for total return with emphasis on maintenance of purchasing power. Do not distinguish between income and principal.
5. Avoid parochial or provincial investing. Some world markets, other than U.S. markets, may have greater investment appeal and should be explored.

When these rules are followed, the committee will be better structured to succeed.

If I could find an institution to accept these guidelines, at least it would help to correct its investment posture, and I would be ready to work in its behalf.

THE LEWIS AND CLARK EXPEDITION

What do you think it would cost today to send a trained team of forty men into an unexplored wilderness for two years? Such an expedition might cost billions of dollars if space exploration in the 20th Century is any guide.

Yet less than two hundred years ago, Thomas Jefferson requested an appropriation from Congress for such a venture. Two resourceful frontiersmen, at Jefferson's instructions, led forty men on a journey from the mouth of the Missouri River to the Columbia River in 1804. They returned in 1806. For this remarkable mission, the Federal Government appropriated the sum of two thousand five hundred dollars. What is more, the expedition was successfully completed within budget and without loss of life.

This achievement of Lewis and Clark encourages me to explore a much more traveled territory. I am determined to look at the hazardous terrain of the investment landscape of the nineties and to search for opportunities. I ask any who desire to come along to bring an open mind and a trace of optimism. This may offset the difficult nature of the trip.

You won't be surprised to find most of the journey has been already traveled. On our way we have noted the irresponsible increases of debt like rising rivers from melting snow and have seen the steady erosion of the purchasing power of the dollar. We have seen inflation eating away at our provisions like an economic carnivore poised to take larger and larger bites of our provisions.

As your self-appointed scout, I am determined to escape these rising rivers and to leave comfort, and to seek a land inhabited by natives whose possessions are growing in value not eaten away. I think I know such a place. Grab your wallet.

The rapid changes that are occuring in underveloped countries, nations that are more properly characterized today as emerging nations has to amaze you.

I haven't visited many of them, but I plan to. The statistics I have been reading lead me to believe these countries are investment opportunities no farther away than the New York Stock Exchange. Over fifty foreign country funds are listed on the New York Stock Exchange.

The nations that intrigue me include places with rising incomes, slowing inflation rates, hard working people, and evidence of economic controls, with moderating debt levels. There really are such lands.

In past years, these were unfriendly shores, poverty-stricken environments that seemed destined to remain primitive; Malaysia, Taiwan, Thailand, Singapore, Mexico and Spain were some. Their wage rates today are low by any western standards and their people seem inspired to make the things the Western World and Japan have so long produced.

In the fullness of time I shall list the statistics that reveal my reasons for optimism. I shall summarize the important factors. But not right now. It is enough for me to suggest that any investment portfolio for the nineties is probably incomplete without a commitment abroad in emerging nations. I am on my way to explore them and to write another book.

Meanwhile, avoid instinctive prejudice, question seriously your prior investment habits, look realistically even critically at the landscape that now holds your attention and decide to reconsider. If the emerging nations don't deserve your consideration, stay. I shall make the journey without you.

If you are prepared to go, keep reading my books and watch for the postman. In time I'll reveal all the most attractive areas for investment for your consideration.

And meanwhile, avoid debt.

INNOCENCE ABROAD

You won't believe what happened. I had just drafted my final chapter to this book about investing for the 1990's in foreign lands when I read the Sunday New York Times. There, on the front page of the business section, was an article fully explaining all the closely guarded secrets I had been describing. The piece was entitled "Learning To Love Those Foreign Markets." It told of the large amounts of money going abroad from America. I must say I was disappointed.

But I recovered a bit when I read further that most of the money was invested in Western Europe and Japan, not much in the emerging nations. So there may still be time.

Now, I feel better. I feel like an explorer again, on an expedition that rivals Lewis and Clark.

I'll write.

IN PASSING

The final chapter of my book has to be a discussion of my estate plan in case I die and I don't go exploring. Then who will go in my place? I have always thought people spent too much time trying to invest while they are living and too little time planning the investment of their funds after they die.

I am not about to leave my wealth to a bank "trussed" department.

So I thought as a final exertion, I'd disclose my estate plan, hoping that you would respond by appointing me your executor.

When I first moved my family to New Canaan, Connecticut, I was introduced to Mabel Lamb, a realtor. I purchased a home through Mabel that to my mind was and is still the prettiest home in Connecticut. I mention this incident because Mrs. Lamb unknowingly had something to do with the content of my last will and testament.

Mabel had two nieces, her only heirs, who both had important careers. She wanted to leave everything to them but did not wish to detract them from their professional work.

She decided to leave her estate in trust with the income distributed to the nieces according to their earned income. The more they earned, the more they received from the estate. In her words, she wanted to give them an incentive to work harder, to earn more.

I have often thought about Mabel's estate plan. It has caused me to tell of mine.

My residence in Florida is held jointly with my wife and goes to her if I predecease her without probate delay or tax impact.

My tangible personal property also goes to her, except certain items I have (by written memorandum) given to my friends and my children.

In all other financial respects, my wife is already financially provided for.

My intangible property, which is everything else I own, has already recently been placed in an *inter vivos* trust; I am the trustee. During my lifetime, I can do anything I could do as before, including the right to terminate the trust. No accounting is required. On my death, the successor trustee named is my young partner in Greenwich, if he survives me; and my other partner, if he does not. Both of these men are twenty years my junior and are successors to an investment firm the three of us established twelve years ago.

This *inter vivos* trust permits the passing of the investment problems of my estate, the instant I die, to qualified, trustworthy managers; there is no probate delay and no executors fees on these assets.

The trust instrument provides the trustee the widest possible investment powers.

Title to the securities is not encumbered by the trust instrument during my lifetime nor after my death. A copy of the trust instrument is held at each brokerage office where securities are traded as a legal formality.

The trust provides that the corpus, as well as other financial assets which I may be entitled to from my profit sharing and pension plan in my firm, will be divided into as many equal parts as I have children (five). The income is to be paid quarterly to each of them, but there is no requirement that the corpus be run to maximize yield. To offset any shortfall in yield to my beneficiaries, the successor trustee can invade principal in his sole discretion for any child of mine as he deems appropriate.

Each child has a power of appointment to dispose of his share of the corpus at his death to his surviving spouse or his children as he decides. If he fails to do so (or if he is not married and childless) his share goes to his heirs by intestate succession.

While there is nothing in this plan that avoids applicable State and Federal estate taxes, all the obvious tax saving features have been employed. Frankly, there aren't many.

Three principal objectives have been achieved by this plan: First, I have eliminated executors fees and probate costs. The bulk of my estate is intangible property, all of which is in the *inter vivos* trust. Second, there are no bank trustees. In my lifetime, lawyers and bankers have contributed more to high costs and poor investment results than any other professional class. Thirdly, the trust is not run for the income beneficiaries. Yield on the portfolio is ignored. Only total return is emphasized. NO municipals!

If at my death, I am fortunate enough to leave a very large estate (which I doubt), I have placed a cap on the size of the children's trusts, anything in excess to go to a college in Claremont, California.

This clause, I hope, will assure my beneficiaries adequate income, but not so much that it will destroy their incentive to earn as much as possible; to work hard. I have never known a legatee whose interest was served by a large bequest. I have known many where the reverse was the case.

The residuary gift to the college, I believe, is a better method of disposition of charitable funds than the creation of a family foundation. I have been involved with many family foundations and have never seen one that was well run. Most foundation board members are family or friends, rarely are any of them qualified.

Rarely have any of them suffered the "advantages of poverty."

I have found family foundations a source of unnecessary friction and family feuds. In addition, Federal tax laws encourage a high yield investment policy for all foundations which, to me, is tantamount to low net returns.

The college of my choice is small and emphasizes engineering, math, and science courses. I consider this type curriculum better preparation for young people than liberal arts.

That's my estate plan, nothing dramatic or exciting, but I thought I'd mention it in passing.